A Pollack

Penguin Books
Death of The Lucky Co

Donald Horne is one of Aust
critics. In the last twenty years he has done a lot of
editing, including the Sydney *Observer*, *Quadrant* and
the *Bulletin* (twice); he is now Senior Lecturer in
Australian Politics at the University of New South
Wales and a contributing editor to *Newsweek
International*. He has contributed his own informed
brand of analysis and interpretation to many magazines
and newspapers, both foreign and Australian. Since
writing *The Lucky Country* (a phrase which has passed
into common usage, but not always with the author's
intended ironies) he has written *The Permit*, *The
Education of Young Donald*, *God is an Englishman*, *The
Next Australia*, *But What If There Are No Pelicans?* and
The Australian People. He is married with two children,
and lives in Sydney.

Death of The Lucky Country

Donald Horne

Penguin Books

Penguin Books Ltd,
Harmondsworth, Middlesex, England
Penguin Books Inc.,
7110 Ambassador Road, Baltimore, Maryland 21207, U.S.A.
Penguin Books Australia Ltd,
Ringwood, Victoria, Australia
Penguin Books Canada Ltd,
41 Steelcase Road West, Markham, Ontario, Canada
Penguin Books (N.Z.) Ltd,
182-190 Wairau Road, Auckland 10, New Zealand

First published in Penguin Books 1976
Reprinted 1976

Copyright © Donald Horne, 1976

Made and printed in Australia at
The Dominion Press, Blackburn, Victoria

Set in Intertype Plantin by The Type Shop, Melbourne

CIP

National Library of Australia
Cataloguing in Publication data

Horne, Donald Richmond, 1921–
Death of the lucky country.

ISBN 0 14 070049 8

1. Australia. Parliament - Elections - 1975
2. Australia - Politics and government - 1975-
I. Title

994.06

Contents

Thanks

My wife, Myfanwy, has helped with all my books, but since this one was done in three and a half weeks' convalescence after an eye operation, I couldn't have written it without her assistance in everything from detailed editing to matters of logistics. I must also thank the skill of the surgeons and the efficiency of the nursing staff at the Sydney Eye Hospital.

A number of other people helped in reading drafts and proofs, providing ideas, acting as sounding boards. Thanks to them all – and also to Susie Roth, Eryl Brady and Libi Nugent for such fast and willing typing, most of it done over the Christmas-New Year holiday period, and to Julia and Nicholas Horne, for their assistance.

References to figures for preferred votes came from Malcolm Mackerras's *Election 1975* (Angus & Robertson).

One

Landscape of Disaster

By the time I got out of the bus at Martin Place, on Wednesday, the third day of the 1975 election campaign, it was obvious that the retina was buckling at the back of my right eye: there was a grey patch in the vision of the inner corner. I bought a copy of the *Bulletin* at a news stand and began reading the piece I had written – 'Why I wouldn't vote for Malcolm Fraser'. Then I looked for the Morgan Gallup Poll in the *Bulletin*. I had heard about it the Friday before at Tony's Bon Gout, a restaurant associated with the Whitlam years, at which I had said that if Whitlam won the election I would cry in front of the television set. In victory one should cry, because of the perils of success; one should laugh in defeat. A friend said I'd better start laughing: next week's Gallup Poll in the *Bulletin* was going to show that after the Governor-General dismissed the Whitlam government the swing had gone strongly to the Liberals. The Whitlam government had been sacked by an official it had itself appointed who showed his difference from other people by the number of times he wore striped trousers and top hat, and the voters – or a significant margin of them – had accepted his action. Now in the doctor's waiting room I read the detailed poll figures. It was true. The hour of glory had not arrived. The people had not responded. I shut my left eye and with my right looked at the page: the grey blindness had spread half across the eye. Now the figures were obscured. That was better.

I was to have the night at home resting before they admitted me to the Eye Hospital the next morning. I would then spend twenty-four hours with both eyes blindfolded, then they would operate and try, by draining fluids and scarifying tissue, to put the retina back where it belonged. Later, they would weld it with laser beams. My wife and I went through the list of things-to-do I had scribbled out on the back of the *Bulletin* while I was at the doctor's surgery. There was only a sliver of vision in the far right of the eye now. When we finished with the list I shut my eyes and imagined what it might mean if the poll figures accurately represented a significant mood. Humiliatingly, the suggestions they made at Tony's Bon Gout might be right: there were enough authority-respecting Australians for them to change sides when a Governor-General had spoken. Australia was still colonial enough for the will of Government House to prevail. Alternatively there was the pragmatists' theory of the hip-pocket nerve: when the Senate was using the blocking of the supply of money to force the government into an election, support had swung to Labor because people felt their incomes threatened. Now that there was to be an election the hard heads had swung back to the Liberals, thinking there was money in it for them. (Which would show them to be as stupid as hard heads often are.) Perhaps, because of this marginal shift, the Australian people were about to betray what might have been their destiny: positively affirming themselves a nation self-confident in its democratic forms. Two nights later, delirious as I recovered from the anaesthetic, I struggled with the nurses and my wife, on and on, for a couple of hours. I knew they had me in a cage. Downstairs were the documents that would prove the Morgan Gallup Poll was wrong. They wouldn't let me go down and clear the name of the Australian people. Later, at midnight, when I had re-orientated myself as a hospital patient, and one who had to accept the Morgan Gallup Poll, the nursing sister wrote on the post-operative report that the patient was 'conscious, co-operative, vague'.

In the tunnel of darkness in which I lived for eleven days, as well as cassette music of Handel, Haydn and other positive thinkers, I heard all the radio news, listening for more opinion polls. I rang my wife after breakfast each morning: was there any good news yet in the polls? I had a new theory: the Liberals' concentration on the economy as the main issue of the election would bounce back on them. During the campaign a significant margin of the hard heads would detect the fraudulence of the idea that the economic crisis was simply due to either Labor's 'bad management' or its 'socialism' and that once the Liberals took over, the crisis would go away and 'prosperity would be restored'. On the day before the election I came out of hospital into the glare of a heat wave. A band of dock workers, banners calling for Labor for Australia, marched along the road on their way to a rally. A policeman was with them, to stop the traffic at intersections. We bought an afternoon paper. The opinion polls were as bad as ever.

While I was in hospital I decided that if the frauds did work, if there was to be success for the most sustained and corrupting campaign to destroy a government in our national history, with outrages committed against the decencies of our political life, a huge campaign of political misrepresentation and a vendetta journalism so virulent that it makes me ashamed to have been a journalist, then I should write a book giving meaning to these events and suggesting some of the puzzles that have been cast into the future.

The day Whitlam was sacked he said to the crowd on the steps of Parliament House: 'Maintain your rage'. If you felt rage at the time this book is intended to help justify it; and, if you did not feel rage then, to understand and now perhaps join with those who did.

The book is addressed in part to that coalition of Labor supporters and concerned people who were deeply motivated during the December 13 election campaign. But it is also addressed to those other Australians who may have taken another side at the time, but who share similar principles and priorities. Those who voted Labor may see more clearly how they were robbed. Those who voted Liberal may begin to

11

understand how they were misled. For both, the book may help crystallize common feeling and a new consciousness of politics in Australia.

The book is not intended to be wholly or mainly polemical, although there should be no shame in writing spiritedly. It is intended to throw up the shapes of what have been dark and sometimes unexamined aspects of Australian political life, and to look into matters that might previously not have seemed worth investigating. After the sense of atrocity suffered by so many Australians, we have to learn to see our politics in a new way.

What happened?

This: The Governor-General secretly made a decision, the effect of which was to support the political plans of the Liberal and National Country Parties.

Against all contemporary practice he did not discuss that decision with the government that was then in power. But having contemplated the decision secretly he secretly got for it the support of the Chief Justice, a person of no more constitutional significance in this matter than you or me, but one whose respected office could seem to give extra authority to what the Governor-General had decided. The Governor-General then mounted a time-tabled operation, for which the phrase 'constitutional *coup d'état*' seems a useful description. It was an operation which had the general effect of leaving the Prime Minister with a false sense of security, then, without discussing any alternatives, kicking him out of office, installing the minority leader as Prime Minister, then dissolving Parliament. It all happened so quickly that no preventive action could be taken.

What were the political effects of this action?

It got the Liberal and National Country Parties a chance to fight an election at a time that suited them, and under circumstances that favoured them quite extraordinarily. After the constitutional *coup d'état* the quick plebiscitary election was conducted in unparalleled circumstances in which Labor could seem a guilty party dismissed by rightful authority. This impression could have been strengthened by a continuing campaign of 'revelations' none of which was to be substantiated. An unfair electoral system magnified the swing. In the House of Representatives, with 43.4% of the preferred votes, Labor won only 28% of the seats while the coalition parties with 56.6% of the preferred votes, gained 72% of the seats. In 1966 Labor won only 43.1% of the votes, but gained 34% of the seats. In the Senate the coalition parties gained such a majority that even if Labor wins the next election it cannot control the Senate; in such an event the coalition parties could use their Senate majority to prevent the reform of unjust electoral boundaries and then at a favourable moment sack another Labor government and start all over again.

Yet if the Governor-General had taken the advice the Prime Minister had intended to give him – Whitlam's advice to hold a half-Senate election was demonstrably constitutional – a different kind of election would have been fought, under different circumstances. The Labor Party might have won it. If a general election had been held at some other time, the Labor Party might have won it, or even if the coalition parties had gained a narrow majority in the House of Representatives they may have lacked control of the Senate.

In pointing out that the Governor-General's action gave the Opposition parties the election that best suited their interests and that was most likely to destroy the Labor Party I am not discussing whether the Governor-General had thought about the effects of his actions. Perhaps he did. Perhaps he didn't. I am not suggesting that he intended to give the coalition parties an extraordinary political advantage. Nor can I suggest he didn't, since the motives of a Governor-General are not examinable. What one can say is that, whatever his intentions, never before has an Australian Governor-General intervened in a way that so much favoured one party and so threatened another.

Consider some of the ways in which the Governor-General's action had the effect of favouring Labor's political opponents.

One of the most important was that the Whitlam government was going through a change in character that might have kept it in office if the next election had been held at the normal time, at the end of 1976 or in the first half of 1977. It was in the coalition parties' interests to bring Labor down before this change could be demonstrated. In three years Labor had produced many great achievements; it had also produced many blunders, as might have been expected of a party that had been out of office for twenty-three years; but ironically, just as the follies of its petrodollar dealings with Khemlani received their greatest publicity, the government looked to have a new pragmatism and efficiency. It had become seasoned. It had been a reform government that was patchy in general administration; now it was a reform government that might seem more competent in administration than its rivals, who also had their own follies and blunders.

Labor had blundered in economic management (as the Liberals had in 1971 and 1972) but by 1974 there was a world economic crisis of a new, puzzling kind in which there were no more certainties and the consequences of mistakes were unusually magnified. If things went wrong, they went wrong on a grander scale. If they had won the 1972 or the 1974 elections the Liberals would also have suffered from this magnifying effect. But by the second half of 1975, the Labor government was adjusting itself to these new circumstances. A few months free of political crisis and Labor's economic ministers might have been seen by a significant margin of voters as economic managers who were sounder (as well as more humane) than the Opposition was likely to be. For the

Liberals it was vital that Labor should not have time to do this. Some Liberals had developed such belief in the strategies of Labor's Treasurer Bill Hayden that they wanted to win an election to gain the benefit of these strategies.

The Governor-General's action got Malcolm Fraser off the hook. Fraser's tactic had been to use his political majority in the Senate to cut off the government's money supply and so force an election. This tactic seemed to be failing. It had aroused public antipathy – the opinion polls showed a swing to Labor – and it was being attacked inside his own party. If the game of parliamentary bluff and counter-bluff had been played out, Fraser might have surrendered. Whatever the Governor-General's intention, his intervention saved Fraser from a reckless failure that could have led his party to sack him as leader.

For authority-respecting, innocent-minded voters the drama of dismissing Whitlam and putting Fraser in as Prime Minister could seem an act of punishment for a government that had done wrong. Such voters might see the election as under vice-regal patronage. In itself that may directly have influenced votes. The drama of dismissal certainly pushed Whitlam fatally off his stride. He was pulled away from most of the team he was used to working with, and pushed into sudden improvisations, many of which didn't come off. The Labor team was fractured: it broke into disconnected parts; in some cases they were seriously distracted by the caretaker government's reducing their staff and even by such banalities as attempts to remove office equipment.

The incoherence of the crisis meant that voters barely noticed that Fraser was opening and shutting his mouth without saying anything much. He evaded the questions of media interviewers, slipping off into the magic words of the campaign: 'extravagance', 'international safaris', 'jobs for the boys', 'dole bludgers', 'private sector'; and all the newspaper managers seemed determined to give him an easy run home.

The election came and went without voters realizing they had put Fraser in power without knowing anything much about him or his plans. The sensationalism of this extraordinary election made it, in policies and programmes, remarkably brainless, but remarkably suited to a party that, not wanting its credibility tested, had a vested interest in brainlessness.

Perhaps the greatest scandal was that Labor supporters and those who, more generally, saw themselves as supporters of reform, could see the political set-up stripped of its legitimacy. It could seem as if reformers were not accepted by the Australian political system. They might be tolerated for a while; but they were easily outlawed. For some this was reduced to the simple conspiracy theory of a CIA coup, as in Chile. For others there was the diffused shock of an affronted trust in which they felt that the democratic decencies were not for Australia. The political system seemed to have powerful devices available only to the opponents of reform. In a showdown the reformers could see the system as stacked against them.

In a community like Australia people usually accept political defeat as legitimate because they imagine that some other time they might win. During the twenty-three years of Liberal rule Labor people still saw themselves as part of the set-up. The media was usually against Labor. The electoral system favoured the Liberals. (Labor won an outright majority of votes in the 1954 election, and a majority of preferred votes in the 1961 and 1969 elections, although they didn't get a House of Representatives majority.) But Labor people could still see how they might win.

Under Menzies certain people despised Australia because Menzies was its leader; under Whitlam other people, like White Russians, felt dispossessed. But in either case there could still be a feeling that their time would come again: their own lot would get back in. The campaign to destroy the Whitlam government went on for so long, involved so many powerful institutions, and had such an infamous victory that many people who believed in reform believed it possible that their time would not come again. There was too much power on the other side. They could never win.

To the Labor government supporters, or to those who came to its support because the destruction of the government affronted them, the sacking of Whitlam had the shock of an assassination. It was followed by a dream-like period of physical disorientation: when the words 'prime minister' came over transistors or television sets people still saw the face of Gough Whitlam. They would wake up in the mornings and for a moment imagine it hadn't happened. As the election caravans moved across the landscape of disaster the media put up such a brutal clatter that the sense of shock became sharper. Has there ever been such a crying on an Australian election night? It was not only the Labor Party that was being destroyed, but the sense of trust of hundreds of thousands of Australians.

The Divine Right of the Liberals

Someone in one of the North Shore branches of the Liberal Party had liked a piece I had done for the *Bulletin*. It was written in the week when the Khemlani loans fiasco had reached its most absurd dimensions but I had come out suggesting that there was nevertheless more good in Labor than in its unreformed opponents: I had tried to put Australian politics into a context more general than the daily excitement of the headline and the photostat. It was pleasing that I was asked to address a Liberal branch but when we settled the date we didn't know that it would be during the marshalling of an election campaign. What initially had seemed merely a 'controversial' talk became, in the context of an election, a stick of dynamite which unearthed a representative sampling of Liberal Party rubbish. My attempt to speak of Australia's economic crisis as part of a world economic crisis was seen as Labor electioneering. There I stood, in the Congregational church hall, taunted with bits of Liberal Party dogma.

To recall these attacks (most, to be fair, delivered with politeness, but not all of them) is to summarize a whole strain of Liberal fundamentalism, and for some Liberals the 1975 election was a declaration of a return to basic faiths, which are, however, no longer relevant to our present circumstances. One speaker said unemployment was caused by pampered dole bludgers who needed more discipline. Another said free enterprise must be liberated by making tariffs higher. Someone else said free enterprise would prevail only with strong government leadership. One old man called for a return to the verities of when Australia lived on the sheep's back. Another old man held up a book and asked me if I had read it: it was, he said, on the evils of communism. (I told him I might have written it.) Labor's 'socialism' was attacked by speaker after speaker. The phrase 'free enterprise' was passed from mouth to mouth like a magic charm. It was thought ridiculous to suggest that a world economic crisis affected Australia. Stimulate business confidence and all would be well. One said there had to be a court of appeal (the Senate) against the tyrannies of any elected Labor government which would merely have a 'transient majority'. At coffee time, Labor was attacked as pro-communist and I was attacked as anti-British. One man said to me: 'You're a great Australian patriot. Well I'll tell you what I think of your lucky country. I've got to pay forty per cent tax on the pittance I live on so that the government can buy "Blue Poles" and educate workers' children. So far as I'm concerned you can tow your lucky country into the Indian Ocean and sink it.' When someone else said that the world was divided into good and evil, south and north, Fraser and Whitlam, it took a moment or two for me to recognize that he was merely a conventional religious nut.

The simple faith of 'free' enterprise is, with leftovers from the old imperial imagination, traditional intellectual sustenance for the Liberal and National Country Parties. The economic faith is expressed in primitivist small shopkeeper abstractions ('independence', 'thrift', 'initiative') which do not denote the realities of a complex economic society. In fact the Australian economy would collapse without extensive government support and without the activities of large corporations. Nevertheless expressions of these shopkeeper abstractions have the flavour of religious conviction. The word 'profit' is seen as the magical explanation for what is good in life. Welfare is seen as sapping the individual will. To this the Country Party adds belief in the sacred character of all farming industry whether efficient or inefficient. As heirs of the British Empire the conservative parties have traditionally been citadels of White Anglo-Saxon Protestant respectability; because they believe they have had a monopoly on 'loyalty', first to Britain, then to the United States, they have also believed themselves the guardians of foreign and defence policy. Yet their governments' peacetime defence policies have been outstandingly incompetent; one of Australia's most successful political hoaxes has been the presentation of the coalition parties as good at defence. It was significant that the first initiative in defence planning taken by the Fraser government was to restore the school cadets.

But as well as the economic and imperial faiths, the non-Labor parties have had a self-belief that in sheer power terms has been their most important characteristic: the coalition parties, the Liberals in particular, see themselves as the natural government of Australia. The Irish melancholy of the Labor Party, or the delights of leftwing martyrdom, or the sheer comfort of safe seats can make Opposition not only consoling, but attractive, to some Labor members, but the Liberals always want to get in and win. They have tried (and often succeeded) to establish a monopoly on political legitimacy.

It was the Liberal Party's belief in its divine right to govern that has now caused such disruption of Australian political life. Despite the fuss among the faithful in the Liberal branches, not all Liberal Members of Parliament thought Whitlam's government radical. In fact many were anxious to imitate his 'trendiness'. It was the existence of a Labor government that affronted them more than its policies. It was unnatural for Labor to be in office. In 1974, when they thought they had Labor in a corner, they forced an election. After their defeat they were content to let the government run on: things looked bad – let Labor take the blame. But when Labor showed signs of a recovery the Liberals struck again, in a political cataclysm which would, they hoped, put them back into power for election after election.

In a campaign Labor can depend on the union movement (more or less), some intellectuals, some welfare supporters,

20

some groups of other 'concerned people'. It used also to depend on the Catholic Church, but now it can't. The Liberals, at their strongest, can reinforce their confidence in themselves as the natural government with much more effective institutional support than comes to Labor. Labor imagines itself toppling governments by parliamentary exposure, programmes, open campaigns. (I am speaking here only of the national Labor Party: State Labor Parties can be quite different.) The Liberals imagine themselves getting into power by fixing the support of strong institutions. They have done this three times, in 1931, in 1949, in 1975.

The reliance on business used to be unconcealed: the conservative parties that preceded the Liberal Party were financed by separate money-making groups of businessmen. The Liberal Party is now more democratically organized and independent, but its relations with big business, or big business organizations, can still be very direct, and, at one of the in-to-kill elections, it can be overwhelming compared with the selective support business gives Labor in bad years. At different times Liberal manoeuvrings have been supported not only by business but by political-legal networks (including judges as well as barristers), professional groups, especially doctors, the ex-servicemen's organizations (as in the New Guard during the Depression), much of the intelligence community, including parts of the Australian Security Intelligence Organization, the banks, the media, the 'establishments' of the city clubs; it also draws support from many officers in the armed services.

On the face of it, Labor has great strength in the support given to it by the union movement. But in a liberal-democratic mixed-economy society this is a strength Labor cannot use. If it called a political strike it would lose the next election. The Liberals have a strength they can use. Australia belongs to them more than it does to Labor.

Some political critics regret the absence of an 'intellectual conservatism' in Australia; but except among speech-writers and other pill-sweeteners, such conservatism would get in the way of conservative parties that are so manipulative. In the 1975 crisis many individual Liberal Party members felt pangs of conscience about the ruthless methods used: they were concerned with proper respect for conservative principles; but those engaged in the manoeuvres of the big fix had no doubt about their propriety: whatever they did was proper, because theirs was the right to rule.

The rhetoric of the non-Labor parties in their claims to legitimacy has been one reason why almost all other liberal-democratic mixed-economy nations (that is to say, the western democracies) have seen Australia so often as stodgy and timid.

The repertoire of these claims was put together in the first twenty-five years of this century. It began with the 'Anti-Socialist' alliance of 1905, formed to fight the 1906 election. It was then that the great theme of freedom versus a socialism 'worse than the horrors of the French Revolution' was developed. The words used in 1906 were no different from those the North Shore Liberals used in the 1975 election. Their special magic is to make 'anti-socialists' appear the defenders of the natural order. In the 1917 election two other great themes matured. One was that the Labor Party was under the influence of a secret junta of extremists, a 'secret executive' of 'socialists and agitators' and this stopped it from being a truly national party; the other was that the Labor Party was unnaturally disloyal to a great and powerful friend – 'violently hostile to Britain, sneering at the Empire and all it stands for'. In the 1919 election these two themes reached perfection when they became specific charges that Labor was communist: the forces behind Labor were 'sinister and alien', 'a damned lot of traitors' – 'the Labor Party has gone Bolshevik', its foreign policy was 'to turn to Moscow rather than London'. In the

1925 election the great theme emerged fully developed: the anti-Labor parties were the natural protectors of law and order against industrial anarchy. Now all the tricks were in the bag. They were to continue to be useful for the next fifty years.

This repertoire of horror campaigns which can make the non-Labor parties seem the only proper political parties has not been matched by Labor. Labor has not usually been able to turn attacks on 'monopolies', 'international finance', 'big business', 'the profit motive', or whatever the current scare phrase might be, into efficient political devices, although the word 'multinationals' had some credibility in the 1972 election; and Labor has not usually won votes as a nationalist party that contrasts itself with the imperialists who practise subservience to powerful friends – although it did so in 1941, when it took over running wartime Australia because its opponents, despite their imperialism, had proved in wartime to be politically incompetent. There was also a touch of greater national independence in the 1972 campaign. While its opponents make political capital of the ideology of a 'free enterprise' that does not exist (Australia's economy is a mixture of government and private initiatives, the latter often dependent on the former) it would be to Labor's electoral disadvantage to use the rhetoric of a 'socialism' that does not exist and in which, in the main, it does not believe: the 'socialization objective' of Labor's official platform is highly selective and since the 1975 Labor conference in Terrigal an official Labor objective is also a 'mixed economy'.

Labor has won government as it did in 1929, 1941 and 1972 when the other side had collapsed or looked close to collapse: it was to lose those governments – in 1931, 1949 and 1975 – in horror campaigns orchestrated by various powerful institutions in the community. Labor has usually run cleaner, more rational election campaigns than the other parties. This may not be because of purer-mindedness; it may be that Labor hasn't found such effective devices for tricking people. But for the Liberal Party and its predecessors a natural process of elections is to decide which tricks they will work next.

In the 1975 election campaign as soon as Fraser became caretaker Prime Minister he sensationally accused Labor Treasurer Bill Hayden of stealing files and Gough Whitlam of concealing facts about the economy. In the McCarthyist manner he substantiated neither of these accusations. He simply passed on to another 'revelation' – based on a secret document from the Organization for Economic Co-operation and Development in which he read what proved to be the wrong figures. Once again there was no retraction. Then Alan Reid produced an accusation in the *Bulletin* about the loans affair and the Liberals used it to create another diversion. This was denied by Labor, but from the safety of the Queensland Parliament in the worst single trick of the campaign, extending the parameters of decency so that by comparison Fraser looked a model of purity, Bjelke-Petersen suggested that two Labor Ministers were in for kickbacks in the loans affair: no names, no charges, but another diversion.

Throughout the campaign 'revelation' followed 'revelation'. None was substantiated, but they may have given voters the idea that Labor ministers were crooks; at least, by creating diversions, they kept Whitlam off his stride, and helped Fraser evade media questioning. One of the sad memories of the campaign was listening in my hospital darkness to the Bjelke-Petersen black comedy on the transistor, then listening to a Labor Party friend sitting somewhere in the light outside my bandages, tell me that, yes, the Labor Party had buckets of revelations to tip on the Liberals, but nobody was going to say Labor wasn't fighting a clean election.

There are times when the Liberals run out of effective tricks (every ten or twenty years). 1972 was one of them. Four devices were made ready. None worked. One was the old card of 'defence and foreign policy', but it dropped out of Bill McMahon's sleeve in an interview in Indonesia and Whitlam trumped it anyway with what was to prove a more 'natural' policy (one more like America's) on China than McMahon's. Another card was 'industrial anarchy'. McMahon's attempt to play the strong man in the oil industry strike bounced back; so did the suggestion that ACTU President Bob Hawke was the real ruler of the Labor Party. Some of the murkier Liberal supporters plotted a whispering campaign that Labor would flood the country with Asians, but the Liberal minister Don Chipp sabotaged this, saying that he would like to see an Australia that was 'the only true multi-racial society in the world'. However this did not stop New South Wales Premier Askin from accusing Labor of wanting to 'flood the country with black people'. The fourth trick was that of anti-permissiveness. The Democratic Labor Party made the permissive society a bigger issue than communism, but the Liberals did not take it up until the last desperate week of that election. By then scarcely anyone noticed.

In 1975 there was no floundering. In the battle for the issues (which is what election campaigns are about) the old Liberal devices of 'anti-socialism' and respectability won by a landslide. I would guess that for Labor voters the issues were a serious threat to the survival of a Labor government and/or a sense of affront at the brutality of the constitutional *coup d'état* and/or a belief that Labor's programme (including its economic management) was more efficient and/or more humane. But Liberal voters had the old established tricks: freedom versus socialism, protection from communism, belief in Labor crookedness or incompetence, a belief that Labor had single-handed caused the economic crisis, and a desire to side with the royal authority of the white-haired man in the striped trousers and black top hat.

What I have said here about the Liberal Party is not meant to be a description of it. If I was trying to be comprehensive I would talk about it in a number of other ways; the party might then seem more likeable. I haven't been concerned with describing it in full, but with isolating those characteristics of it that are relevant to this book: its ruthless belief in its own right to rule, the powerful devices of its rhetoric, the powerful institutions that can sustain belief.

In the same way if I were writing a description of the Labor Party I would draw it more fully and point to elements that many readers would find unattractive. But that would also be irrelevant. In any case I have spent a significant part of my life criticizing the Labor Party. What is relevant here is that the Labor Party, in national politics at least, may have a lot more stacked against it than it regularly allows for. In its recovery from its present debacle it should allow for this possibility. If it regains office it must consider more seriously how it can command some of the heights of power. Otherwise it may remain a transient party that enjoys a little bit of office every ten or twenty years.

Before the official 1975 election campaign began and when I still had the use of my eyes I was invited to speak at a Labor rally in Sydney's Hyde Park. I had only once before addressed an open air political rally: in my anglophile days, when I opened a fete in an English village for the Conservative Party. On that occasion there were less than 200 people. At the Hyde Park rally there were 10,000. As soon as I decided that I was going fairly well, I slowed down and looked at the crowd. I was recalling what King George V had done to the House of Lords in 1911: faces looked up, friendly and interested. There seemed a feeling of quietness and strength. I realize now that it was not strength. It was innocence. There was too much against them. They were just people. They were bound to lose.

Three

The Myth of the 'Rules'

Each day at the Eye Hospital my wife would read me the newspaper headings and fill out the subjects that hadn't been reported on radio. She described the television political coverage, then read out that day's ads . . . Christians Concerned for Australia, A Group of Ordinary Australian Citizens, 62 Concerned Members of Staff of Tertiary Education Institutions, Teachers for Democracy, 551 Lawyers Believing in Constitutional Government, The Arts for Labor. Then I would listen to the letters to the editor.

Recurrently irritating themes came through my bandages: letters insisting that the Governor-General clearly had the power to destroy Prime Ministers or Parliaments, or that the Senate clearly had the power to reject money bills, or that these were simple rules and the Governor-General was the umpire. A letter written by two professors of politics said: 'What we are, in fact, facing at present is a temporary technical difficulty in the working of our parliamentary system . . . It is only leading constitutionalists who know what they are talking about and whose views demand respect, divided though they may be themselves on the issues.' This made it sound as if politics is an engine that can be mended only by certain kinds of experts; but in politics we all have the right to consider ourselves expert. All that 'constitutionalists' are expert in is that they are technicians in putting up opposing cases. One case may then prevail, but the case that prevails is not necessarily more correct when it is being argued; it becomes correct simply because it prevails.

Voices in the dark; nurses coming and going. Some would talk politics. Like writers of letters to newspapers they saw the

27

written Constitution as a book in which you could find the instructions. But our written Constitution is not a book of rules. Some of what it says is clearly stated, and accepted. It says the House of Representatives can't sit longer than three years. That is a simple statement, and we follow it. But there are other simple statements in the Constitution which we don't follow. The Constitution makes the Governor-General sound like an absolute monarch. It says he can veto a Bill passed by Parliament, or he can send a Bill back to Parliament recommending amendments to it. The Constitution also says the Governor-General can withhold his assent from a Bill and send it on to Queen Elizabeth, who may veto it. Or that Queen Elizabeth can veto a Bill the Governor-General has already signed. What all that means, if you read it literally, is that the Australian Parliament hasn't got the right to make any laws that the Governor-General doesn't like, or that Queen Elizabeth disagrees with. All these vice-regal and royal powers for vetoing laws are quite precisely stated in the Constitution but they do not decide what happens in our political system. If on his own initiative the Governor-General tried to use these 'powers' it would seem such an arbitrary and authoritarian denial of the elected Parliament that the Prime Minister would sack him. Or at least that was assumed until 11 November 1975.

Other statements in the Constitution are clear but are now given wider meaning than the authors of the Constitution could have imagined. The Commonwealth Government was given powers over 'postal, telegraphic, telephone and other like services'. Those words have been interpreted to include control over the programmes of radio and television stations, which did not exist when the Constitution was drafted and could not have been imagined by the people who drafted it. So that radio and television programmes come under government control in a way unimaginable for theatres, newspapers and magazines.

Other statements in the Constitution are not clear. It is not clearly stated that the Senate can defer, or reject, a Bill granting the government money; nor is it clearly stated that it cannot do so. The statements that are made about the Senate can be used to infer (a) that it can reject money Bills but cannot defer them or (b) that it can both defer them and reject them or (c) that it can neither defer them nor reject them.

What perhaps is most remarkable about the Constitution is that it says nothing at all about many of the matters which Australians have seen as fundamental to their political life. It makes no reference to political parties. It does not refer to the existence of a Cabinet. It does not allow for the existence of a Prime Minister.

A 'clear reading' of our Constitution – just looking at the words and forgetting what happens – suggests that it is despotic, not democratic. It is 'clearly' democratic only to a very limited degree: a Senator may not sit for more than six years, a member of the House of Representatives may not sit for more than three years: when their time is up they must have an election. That is the democratic part. But the Constitution says the Governor-General can decide when Parliament will meet, when its sittings will end, and when the House of Representatives will dissolve. On a clear reading Parliament's right to meet could be limited to one day a year. And even when Parliament does meet, all the Bills it passes could be vetoed by the Governor-General.

On the question of the executive – of who runs the administration – the Constitution makes no pretence of democratic provisions. It says the Governor-General is the government of Australia. He is to be advised by an Executive Council. He appoints the members of the Executive Council and he can dismiss them when he chooses. He sets up the government departments. He appoints the Ministers of State. He can dismiss these ministers when he chooses. These ministers become members of the Executive Council but there is nothing in the

Constitution which says that the Governor-General has to appoint only ministers to the Executive Council.

One of the clearest 'powers' of all the 'powers' the Constitution attributes to the Governor-General is that he is Commander-in-Chief of the armed forces of Australia. So far this has not been taken seriously.

There are danger areas in any written Constitution, worn out old bits which, if interpreted according to one version of literalness, would destroy much existing political life; but they are ignored, or re-interpreted to make sense in a modern context so that the words no longer mean what they seem to say. The Australian Constitution has more danger areas than most because it is a colonial Constitution written in terms of monarchic rather than democratic principles: that was the way they talked in the late nineteenth century. But until 11 November 1975, it was not imagined that these danger areas were operative. We simply kept away from them.

The words of the Constitution should be seen as only part of a more general political system. To find out what happens in our politics you don't necessarily look up the Constitution, with its absurd affronts to democratic aspiration. A large part of our politics needs no reference to it. The words of the Constitution only come in here and there: some words are taken to be obsolete; others have been interpreted to fit into what happens.

The test of a new action is not to look up the Constitution and ask questions such as 'Does the Governor-General have this power?' or 'Does the Senate have this power?' The test of a new action comes from two basic questions: 'What are our present political habits?' and 'What would be the possible effects of this proposed action on our present political habits?' There is always an overriding consideration: is this action likely to damage the whole way we go about politics and threaten the legitimacy of the whole political system? If John Kerr did not consider this he so misinterpreted the role of

Governor-General that he should confess his incompetence and resign. If he did consider this there is a wider range of possible reasons for demanding his resignation. What he has done is to put at peril the concept, as Australians have previously understood it, of 'responsible government'.

That may sound an exaggerated statement, a leftover from the election, not something that really happened. Let me explain it as moderately as I can.

There are a number of democratic aspects of life in Australia but when one speaks of 'parliamentary democracy', or 'parliamentary government' one speaks specifically of voting the government into office via the more democratically elected of the two Houses of Parliament. This is a very limited democracy, if you think of democracy as a system of representative government; and if you think of it as a system of participatory government it is not democracy at all. But it is what we have. And it is more democratic than the intervention of a Governor-General.

Some people imagine that we elect Members of Parliament so that they can govern the country. This is not so. Parliament is a debating, fact-finding, legislating body, not a governing body. It talks. It asks questions. It makes laws. But it doesn't run things. Since the affairs of both Houses of Parliament are controlled by political parties the 'debates' that go on when Parliament is making laws are mainly ritualistic occasions, politically important only because individual members of the parties as a whole use them to show off. Parliament is a place where politicians try to make their mark against an opposing party, or within their own parties. Other than that, Parliament, like *This Day Tonight* or the Melbourne *Age* is a way of drawing attention to public issues and providing information.

It is the political parties that matter in a parliamentary democracy. The parties are imperfect democratic devices. But they are the way we organize our politics. This is why the attempted destruction of the Australian Labor Party as described in the first chapter of this book is an affront to our whole political set-up.

Even more remarkable has been the affront to what we call 'parliamentary government' or 'the Westminster model'. In this system the political party or coalition of parties with a majority of votes in 'the Lower House' in Parliament (the House that is more democratically elected) becomes the government. This system of 'responsible government' is different from presidential government as, say, in the United States, where the government is a president elected indirectly by the voters for a fixed term of office.

The system of 'responsible government' is the system that applies to New Zealand, Canada, Japan, Britain, Ireland, West Germany, Belgium, Norway (with modification), Sweden, Austria, Israel. Until 11 November 1975, it was the system that was believed to apply to Australia. It is not a system in which a government is responsible to the two Houses of Parliament. During the election Malcolm Fraser tried to pretend this was so, but what he was describing was the Italian system, in which either House can vote a government out of office. In the system of 'responsible government' only the most democratically elected House, in our case the House of Representatives, can dismiss the government.

This has been universally acknowledged by political scientists in Australia. Here are three examples:

The essential nature of the Commonwealth's working system of executive government comes then, not from the words of the Constitution, but rather from a whole set of the constitutional conventions of responsible government . . . By these conventions the Governor-General commissions the leader of the majority in the House of Representatives – or the leader of one of two or more parties which between them command a majority of seats and have undertaken to work together upon an agreed programme – to provide and lead a

Ministry . . . the Ministry looks to its rank and file supporters in the House of Representatives to sustain it in office.

(L. F. Crisp, *Australian National Government*)

Australia follows the British system of responsible cabinet government. This system requires that the Queen's representative should act on the advice of a cabinet of ministers [who are] members of parliament having the support of the majority party or coalition in the lower house.

(Geoffrey Sawer, *Australian Government Today*)

The government [is] the party which commands a majority in the lower house.

(Hugh V. Emy, *The Politics of Australian Democracy*)

I would like to print dozens more such quotations, as if they were magic incantations, putting things back where they were. That this was the Australian system was so obvious that when a waitress said, as we were having lunch at the University of New South Wales Staff Club on November 11, that Kerr had just sacked Whitlam, we dismissed it as just not possible. She had got it wrong. Listening to the broadcast of the parliamentary debate we discovered *we* were wrong. But when there was a motion of no confidence in Fraser as Prime Minister we thought it would be all right. The Senate had passed the money Bills. Fraser was demonstrated to lack the confidence of the more democratically elected House; by 5.30 Gough Whitlam would again be Prime Minister of Australia. I went home. The radio was on: they said the Whitlam ministers were moving out their files. I thought of Whitlam's face on television, confidently explaining that we followed the Westminster system in which the government was responsible to the People's House; but Kerr, privately, was to decide otherwise.

What are the political science text books supposed to say now?

Four

Government By Caprice: The Senate

When I arrived home on November 11 and heard on an ABC broadcast that ministers in the Whitlam government were loading their personal files on to trucks I sent telegrams to Whitlam, Hawke and Jim McClelland supporting theirs as the legitimate government; then I sent a telegram to Kerr: 'Congratulations on beginning the destruction of the Australian monarchy. That will give you something to think about during your shameful retirement from Australian history.' In my temporary blindness in hospital, partisanship enveloped me like a bandage, and I could hear the partisanship of others – from the transistor, from people in my room, from unionists marching past the hospital. But it was also possible to retain a sense of irony, as in politics one should. If a Labor majority in the Senate had blocked money to a Liberal government (and some Labor people, notably Senator Lionel Murphy, had said that would be proper) the unionists in the street would be shouting out the justifications the coalition parties were using now. Imagine the hysteria of the Liberals if three of their own traditional forms of support – Government House, the Upper House of Parliament and the Constitution – had been used against them.

In spite of my partisanship I could see, from the predictability of my hospital bed, how the disorderliness of politics could seem the result of disease. Why had there been so many follies in both political parties in Australia?

Blunders are natural to politics. But from the late Menzies era onwards, the Liberal and Country Party coalition governments increased their buffoonery because in changing circumstances they didn't know how to behave. Nor, under Calwell, did Labor. With Labor's victory in 1972, there were two other impulses to clownishness: members of a Labor Party that had been out of office for twenty-three years were inept in government; and members of the coalition parties that had been in office for twenty-three years were inept in Opposition. By 1974 there was also the world economic puzzle of 'slumpflation', in which inflation and unemployment occurred at the same time, a combination that wasn't supposed to be possible: under these circumstances nobody – neither Labor nor Liberal – knew how to behave.

Many of the follies that made the biggest headlines were the least important. Most were of no final consequence. Perhaps the longest-lasting folly occurred in April 1974 when the Liberals, the Country Party and the Democratic Labor Party decided to use their combined Senate majority to block the government's money supply and force Whitlam to an election. Twelve months before, in April 1973, only five months after Labor won its December 1972 election, the Country Party was already privately suggesting that the Senate force a new election as there was a chance they might pick up a majority. In October 1973 they went public: a meeting of the party voted to seek an election immediately. 'There is an overwhelming feeling in the electorate that the government has been given long enough', said Doug Anthony, who obviously thought that ten months' office every twenty-three years was good enough for Labor; but the Liberals weren't certain and the DLP said 'no'. Labor was allowed to remain in office until, in April 1974, Opposition Leader Snedden said he was 'not prepared to take the responsibility of allowing the country to continue in the direction it is being taken ... by the Labor socialist government'. Labor was to be allowed eighteen months in office every twenty-three years. Whitlam evaded the Senate threat by calling a double dissolution of both Houses, hoping as the Constitution allows, that if he won the election a joint sitting of both houses would pass the Bills the Senate had rejected. In fact Labor was returned but still without a Senate majority. Its weakness in the Senate allowed the campaign to destroy the government to continue for another eighteen months.

The coalition parties had deliberately walked into one of the danger areas of the Constitution, establishing a situation which can again blow up stable government. For the moment what matters most is that the campaign of destruction since the blunder of the 1974 election has weakened the democratic consensus and corrupted the Australian political system. The Senate itself rejected a revision intended to bring electoral boundaries up to date with population changes and make them somewhat fairer; it did this to preserve the racket that favours the Country Party in the electoral boundaries. It continued the threat of blocking supply, so that for eighteen months the administration of Australia's national affairs was carried out by a government under continuous threat of a sudden election. Contrary to the practice of several decades, State governments in New South Wales and Queensland replaced Labor Senate vacancies with non-Labor Senators: one of these unfair replacements made possible the particular Senate manoeuvre that the Governor-General accepted as reason for dismissing the Whitlam government. If Premier Bjelke-Petersen had replaced the dead Labor Senator Milliner with another Labor Party man, that particular manoeuvre would not have been available.

To estimate the seriousness of this recklessness consider the alternative: the Liberal and Country Parties could have suspended their divine right to rule and spent a full three years as Opposition, using the time to think and to freshen their approaches. An election would have been due in December 1975. They would probably have won it – on fair boundaries, and in a manner accepted by Labor supporters as legitimate, if disappointing. They could have won it on the conciliatory grounds that the Whitlam government had produced reforms but now it was time for consolidation. This is the story they are now spreading: Whitlam tried too much all at once; now the people want things to go more slowly. But to use that argument under the circumstances of the 1975 election is as if a gang of pirates seized a peaceful vessel, slaughtered the crew and then said now everybody was ready for peace and quiet.

Whitlam's crashthrough programme will be lauded in the history of reform. The coalition parties' crashthrough programme to regain office will be chronicled as part of the history of political atrocity and absurdity.

The next chapter will discuss assertions that the Constitution gave the Governor-General no alternative but to dismiss Whitlam. Here I will discuss two justifications of what happened, both related to the Senate: the justification that it was democratic for the Senate to force an election, and the related justification of the Senate as a necessary check on government.

The 'democratic' argument runs: *elections are democratic, so how can democracy be threatened by holding this election?* The answer is: why should the Senate be the body that decides when Australia has elections? The Senate is not an impartial body; it is an institution composed of politicians who use it to their parties' advantage. And as a representative body it is less 'democratic' than the House of Representatives; its method of election means that each State is represented by the same number of Senators so that 400,000 Tasmanians are represented by ten Senators and nearly 5,000,000 people in New South Wales are also represented by ten Senators.

Not that this settles anything. The democratic question about holding an election is whether the people want one. No matter how the Senate is elected its actions will be based on prospects of party advantage. It is not a body that has any particular powers of divination about whether the people want an election; even if it could see into people's minds it would only call for an election if this suited the party interests of a majority of its members. The Senate is not a 'court of appeal', as some coalition propagandists put it; it is simply an instrument of party power.

The people did not appeal to the Senate to hold an election. One of the scandals of 1975 was that there was no evidence that a majority of voters wanted an election. The opinion polls suggested a majority of voters did not want one. Wanting a change of government does not mean wanting a premature election. The people may have been ready to leave the government in office for its full term, and by then the majority might have switched back to supporting the government, or at least the swing might not have been so damaging to Labor. Only the special nature of the election may have produced the landslide; whatever his intention, that is one possible result of the Governor-General's action.

Before this crisis, the position in effect was that the Prime Minister decided when an election would be held. Whether or not the Governor-General should agree just on the Prime Minister's say-so was disputed – some said 'yes', some said 'no' – but it was fairly generally held that with at least a minimum case for an early election, the Governor-General should do what he was told. This was not 'democratic' in the sense of ensuring that an election was held only when the people wanted one. And it could favour the Prime Minister's party. But it was 'democratic' in the sense of leaving control with a responsible government and it minimized the importance of the Governor-General.

For those who believe that an election should be called when the people want one, what remedy is there? Nothing easy. At the beginning of Federation some democrats hoped to install in the Australian Constitution the American ideas of 'initiative and referendum', which give the people the right to propose a law for which a certain percentage of voters petition, and then to vote on it. They also wanted to adopt the idea of 'recall', which gives the people the right to call for an election on the petition of a certain proportion of voters. Those options remain. In fact I don't think they would work. Making government in Australia more representative or giving it some participatory nature might be more difficult than that, but anyway this is too complicated to discuss in this book.

What I am concerned with is that there is nothing 'democratic' in the Senate calling an election to suit the purposes of the politicians who control it, and that the less power a Governor-General has the better. If we want to give the running of our affairs a more democratic aspect it is ludicrous to look to a combination of the Governor-General and the Senate. The reason for arguments for the democratic role of the Senate in the 1975 election was to assert the right of the Liberal and Country Parties, on those rare occasions when the Labor Party had become the government, to use their control of the Senate to force an election when they thought they could win.

The idea that a strong Senate is necessary as a check on the tyranny or the dishonesty or the incompetence of the government is equally spurious. If it is taken from the example of the United States it is simply silly, because the American political system, with its election of the President by the people and the complete separation of the President from Congress, is quite different from the Australian. In any case the American Senate does not have the power to force an election, as John Kerr has now decided the Australian Senate does. The timing of elections is fixed by the American Constitution and there is nothing the Senate can do about it. If the idea of the Senate as a strong check on government is from democratic countries that practise the system of responsible government there is again no case. These countries are Austria, Britain, Belgium, Canada, Ireland, Israel, Japan, New Zealand, Norway, Sweden, West Germany. In three of these there is no Upper House. The Upper Houses in most of the others are specifically prevented from cutting off government money, and where the power theoretically remains it is acknowledged to be fossilized.

There are already two strong legal checks on Australian national governments. If a government does anything that seems beyond its constitutional powers it can be challenged in the High Court of Australia. Or if members of a government do anything that seems illegal they can be charged with their alleged crime and tried in an appropriate court. It is true that there is no unquestioned constitutional method whereby an incompetent government can be dismissed. How could there be? Who would judge a government's competence? Certainly not the Senate, which is either controlled by the governing party, in which case it would never dismiss the government, or is controlled by the government's political opponents, in which case it might dismiss the government any time it thought it had a chance of winning an election. It is usually assumed in liberal-democratic countries that the voters are the only judges of competence and that governments keep this in mind as they govern. There are many questionable assumptions in this, but none requires the existence of an impartial authority able to decide that a government is so incompetent it should be dismissed and an election held.

On the Wednesday before the election, having had a day with one eye unbandaged, I was given laser beam treatment for my right eye. Then again both eyes were covered. Optimistically, I had hired a television set to see 'Light a Candle for Democracy', the Labor rally to be held that evening in Canberra outside Parliament House; the sister had a word with the surgeon, instructions were entered into my file, and the left eye pad was taken off for half an hour so that I could watch. An eye dilated by drops stared through glasses which were pushed too far down my nose by the pad covering the other eye. It stared at a portable television set that shimmered and wavered because the area happens to be one of the worst for television reception in Sydney.

But it was one of those many occasions in the 1975 election when politics were intensified into moral meaning. And such intensification is rare in Australia. It was our Parliament House that framed the rally; our flag. When they sang *Advance Australia Fair* I released a few tears from my left eye on to my cheek and from my right eye into the eyepad, an effect of this banal song I would not previously have expected. Back in bandaged darkness I counted the reasons for optimism – the Wagga by-election, a Latrobe University survey in Diamond Valley, reports from a friend of a successful doorknock in Strathfield, an enthusiastic meeting my mother went to in Mosman. Perhaps the great victory might still come: Kerr would be forced into the retreat from history I had promised in my telegram; the Senate would be reduced to its proper place; an affirmation would be made of a morally self-confident Australia.

The debacle that followed has not been as depressing as I had expected. One hears everywhere of defeated people stirred sufficiently by the election to feel changed, ready to look at things with new consciousness. Given this, I will talk in this chapter and at the end of the next about reforming our Constitution to make it more democratic, something I would not have wasted time on before the extraordinary election of December 13. It might still seem beyond common sense to discuss such an ambition, but common sense might change.

The Senate. If there is still to be a Senate, it should be specifically prevented from rejecting a Bill granting money to the government. But why should it have any rights at all to reject legislation? The Senate was established as a House representing the States, but right from the start it failed in this. It has been simply a House controlled by politicians, but controlled in different and unpredictable proportions from the

41

House of Representatives because of its eccentric method of election. Since it does not guard State interests it has become a House of Review. But what special competence has it got as a House of Review? Why should its judgement be better than that of the House of Representatives?

Do we need an Upper House? I don't think so. New Zealand and Sweden manage without one. Anyway if the Senate is controlled by the same parties as control the House of Representatives it is a mere rubber stamp. But if Australians still want a Senate, why not turn it into a real House of Review with a membership – usually sitting in committee, occasionally sitting as a full chamber – of eminent persons, nominated by the parties, able to call for information and make recommendations, but with no right to make laws? This arrangement might be useful. It might not. But it wouldn't do any harm.

An alternative would be to turn the Senate into a true States' House (and call it that), consisting of delegations of equal size appointed by the State Governments and under instruction from them, with the right to seek information and to make recommendations, but again no power to make laws.

Voting. By 1953 it was beginning to look as if the government of R. G. Menzies, put into power in 1949, and returned in a double dissolution in 1951, might be near its end. In the Senate election of that year Labor won 50.61% of the vote, and the Communists, whose preferences predictably go to Labor, 3.05%. In the House of Representatives election the next year, if you looked simply at the total vote, you would have believed that Labor had won. It got 50.03% of the first preferences and the Communists got 1.24%. Obviously Menzies was out: he had belied his promise and Australians had got sick of him. In fact Menzies was back in. The electoral system had given him more seats than Labor although he got fewer votes. If Labor had won government as well as a majority of votes in 1954 it is possible that the attractions of office would have held together a party that in fact was to split soon after its election victory-defeat; the Liberals might then have replaced Menzies with someone better at getting votes. The electoral system – in 1954, and as I suggested in the first chapter, in 1961 and 1969 – has given an entirely false emphasis to Australians' party choices. Three times during the twenty-three years of continuous Liberal rule Labor, in votes, won elections. A democratic Constitution should guard against such injustice.

Malcolm Mackerras wrote a most important article in the *Bulletin* just before the 1975 election. He pointed to what was, in effect, the class bias of the voting system for the Senate. The argument is that since the level of formal education among Labor voters is, overall, lower than among Liberal voters, the peculiarities of Senate voting work to the disadvantage of Labor in producing more informal votes. In Sydney's reddest-ribboned Labor seat, informal votes for the Senate in the 1974 election were 20.5%; in the bluest-ribboned Liberal seat they were 5.6%. Nearly 800,000 people voted informal. They were virtually disenfranchised and most of them would have been Labor. If they had voted formally Labor would have won control of the Senate in 1974 and Labor would have had a full three years in office. In other words, a class bias in the electoral system destroyed the Labor government. The coalition masters of the Senate blocked legislation that would have made Senate voting easier.

Government By Caprice: The Governor-Generalate

Australia's position is now this: one man, an appointed, not elected, official, can take a decision that changes Australian political life, yet he is entirely unaccountable to us. He is unchallengeable: there is no undoing what he does. We can ask him questions but he won't give us answers. And he is hard to criticize: both conventions of fairness and, in some parts of the media, straight out suppression, protect him.

It is intolerable that such power should be protected by the mystifications of the English crown. During the Khemlani loans affair, I think only the *Australian Financial Review* pointed out that the Governor-General had signed the minutes authorizing Connor to raise multi-billion petrodollar loans for 'temporary purposes'. It might have been expected that an official powerful enough to sack one Prime Minister and put in another would question the constitutionality of these loan raisings before authorizing them. Did he do so? If not, why not? If his argument was that his job was simply to follow the advice of his ministers, why didn't he apply that principle and follow the advice of Gough Whitlam during the Senate crisis?

The real lesson of the loans affair was that our monarchic constitution may be used so that ministers can be authorized to raise multi-billion dollar loans without the Australian people knowing. For those who believe in checks and balances on government actions this situation should seem in need of remedy. But it touches on a matter some may see as more important – the inviolability of the monarchic principle. The real scandal of the loans affair was that billions of dollars might have been secretly raised on the signature of an appointed official. With a more democratic constitution this would not have been possible.

A dinner that Jim McClelland always seems to remember was one at which I urged him, for hours, to stand for the Senate. Another guest at that dinner whom I also urged to go into public life was John Kerr. This came to mind when I read during the Senate crisis that McClelland and Whitlam had had lunch at Government House with Kerr. At this lunch, it is said, Kerr again gave the impression that he would not intervene against Whitlam, but suggested that Fraser might be let off the hook. I don't imagine that McClelland will ever sit down to a meal with John Kerr again.

Of all the political disadvantages that came from Whitlam's crashthrough style of government (there were also, of course, many advantages) the worst was not the Khemlani loans decision, but Whitlam's failure to think about what he was doing before appointing John Kerr to the Governor-Generalship. Whitlam and his staff didn't take the office seriously: they saw it as that of ribbon-cutter and manager of the government guest house. Kerr got on to the short list because he was a knight. They thought that whomever they put in as Governor-General should be a knight, and so, as well as not paying sufficient attention to the possible political powers of the office, they underestimated its symbolic significance: it might be unfair to knights but a nationalist Labor government should have deliberately looked for a Governor-General who was *not* a knight. A government that had decided to dispense no more British honours should have made the gesture of choosing a Governor-General who was a plain 'mister'. And a democratic Labor government should have told its appointee not to wear top hat and morning dress: in Australia this is the costume of the furthest reaches of what considers itself the upper socio-economic class. It was a symbolic assault on Labor's democracy that the Governor-General should dress in the style of the members' stand and the society wedding.

I remember only one good thing from John Kerr's period as Governor-General: he abolished the curtsy. Otherwise he seemed to play the bunyip aristocrat. I remember the first time I saw him dressed up: striped trousers, cutaway coat festooned with baubles and *a black top hat*. In the 1840s in Sydney they had a phrase for the Government House and clubland set – 'the black hats'. Kerr had become a 'black hat'. In saying this I am not sneering at people who change their way of life. I've done so myself several times. But I would sneer at the Australian black hats – the last tatty remains of a failed Australian upper class.

Kerr's black-hattery began with the Labor Party split in 1954. Kerr had built up a big practice at the bar connected with the right-wing industrial group unions. After the Labor Party split, at a house in the Sydney suburb of Ryde, Santamaria offered him the groupers' crown – chairmanship of the about-to-be-formed Democratic Labor Party. He refused; it was the beginning of the slow business of disentangling his practice from the trade unions into other areas of the law. I saw him one day in Martin Place. He had taken to wearing a homburg. He joined the Union Club: he became Chief Justice of New South Wales. In this position he was notable for his administrative work, in which he was a reformer; he didn't write many judgments. (In fact, he has never achieved much regard as a lawyers' lawyer.) But he seemed to have found an honourable way out. If he was going to be a black hat, he might as well do a useful job.

Some old friends wondered why he moved to Government House, from a useful job to a purely ceremonial one. New acquaintances saw him as a jovial host enjoying conversation and conviviality, enjoying being out of the game. I think he may still have seen himself as being in the game. Kerr has been one of those two dozen or so people I knew when young who seemed obviously bound to be Prime Minister of Australia.

(Gough Whitlam was not one of them; he was an undergraduate wit.) This was clear the first time I met him, in 1945. I was a diplomatic cadet; he was a lieutenant-colonel on the staff of Alf Conlon, prince of mysteries and a renowned wartime 'operator'. I remember Kerr, tall, slim, shock of dark hair, full of ideas, selling them to me, one by one. Kerr's own political ambitions failed. He had never seemed ready for the risks of political life. But as Governor-General he was as close to the centre of things as a cautious man could get. As it turned out, his hand was on the hangman's lever.

Some more quotations from political science text books:

As in the case of the Queen his [the Governor-General's] powers are controlled by convention. He acts on the advice of his ministers. As in the case of the Queen, he need not be a cypher, and has 'the right to be consulted, the right to encourage, and the right to warn'.

(Geoffrey Sawer, *Australian Government Today*)

It is accepted that the Governor-General, like the English monarch, is politically neutral and impartial between parties . . . Also, it is accepted that at all times the Governor-General acts on the advice of his ministers; for every action he performs he must have a minister willing to accept responsibility for it before parliament.

(Hugh V. Emy, *The Politics of Australian Democracy*)

The Governor-General, in the early years of the Commonwealth, was able to exercise some power and use some discretion in his own right. The role of the occupant of the position has, however, changed with changes in that of the sovereign so that, today, his authority is exercised almost entirely on the advice of ministers.

(W. J. Byrt and Frank Crean, *Government and Politics in Australia*)

So long as it [the government] retains the confidence of the House of Representatives, the Governor-General will perform official acts only upon the advice of these ministers.

(L. F. Crisp, Australian National Government)

The idea that a Governor-General should not act without a government taking responsibility for his actions pleased the democrats, who saw it as a guarantee against arbitrary intervention. It also pleased those monarchists who believed that the only way of preserving the monarchy was to keep it above politics. It was acceptable irony that in practice the way the monarch or the monarch's representative remained above politics was always to take the side of the governing party. The most extreme example was the support King George V gave to a British reform government in 1911 when the House of Lords blocked a Bill intended to take away its power to refuse money to the government (the very power the Australian Senate first claimed sixty-three years later). On the advice of the government King George smashed the power of the House of Lords to veto money bills by threatening to swamp it with newly created lords. The House of Lords gave in.

The advice Whitlam intended to give the Governor-General on November 11 if the Governor-General had not got in first and sacked him was to call an election for that half of the Senate that was due for election. This was perfectly constitutional advice. Kerr should have let Whitlam give it, then he should have accepted it. An election for half the Senate might have given Whitlam a temporary advantage in the Senate, but if the means were legal, and they should have been, it was no business of Kerr's to question it. Like King George V he should have taken the course suggested by his government. If he had, it is quite likely the Senate would have surrendered.

On the other hand, an election might have left unresolved the deadlock between the Senate and the House of Representatives. So what? The Constitution doesn't state that the Governor-General must solve deadlocks. Deadlocks are political matters of bluff and counter-bluff in which each side

48

plays for public support. One side may give in. If it doesn't, the Constitution (as will be discussed shortly) specifically offers its own way out.

In fact this deadlock may have ended without an election. The indications were that the Liberals were losing public support and were ready to give in. The very least Kerr should have done was to wait another fortnight until the government's money was due to run out. Then the Opposition's bluff would have been called. In prematurely assuming that when the time came the Senate really would continue to cut off supply he acted incompetently because he could not have had that evidence. How could he know what was in the mind of every Senator? That another fortnight's delay would have postponed the elections until late January was no business of John Kerr's. A Governor-General shouldn't threaten the whole system of responsible government in Australia (which is the same as saying the whole system of democratic government in Australia) simply because of convenience. If the Opposition parties had been politically mad enough to cut off supply over the whole summer holiday period they would have been smashed in the subsequent election. But it was not Kerr's job to save the Opposition parties from a self-inflicted defeat. There were even precedents from politics in Victoria in the nineteenth century for a governor *not* to remove a government from office simply because the Upper House had cut off its money.

One of the most curious features is that when Kerr gave the reasons for his actions he seemed to suggest that the Constitution directed him to solve such a deadlock and do it in the way he did. He spoke of his action as a 'constitutional obligation and duty', 'the only solution'. Yet the Constitution explicitly provides a solution for deadlocks. It says that if the Senate rejects a Bill and then three months later rejects it again there can be a dissolution of both Houses of Parliament and a general election. That this might be an inconvenient way out in a crisis over money supply is irrelevant. It is what the Constitution says about breaking deadlocks and Kerr, although referring to the Constitution, did not refer to that part of it.

The Solicitor-General and the Attorney-General, the two principal law officers of the Crown, had advised Kerr a week before he sacked Whitlam that the fact that the Constitution offered a double dissolution to solve a deadlock made questionable the use of 'the reserve power' to sack a government. They suggested that the mere thought of the Senate rejecting supply, or even its actual rejection of it, did not necessarily compel a government to resign. Nor did it compel a Governor-General to intervene. They expressed 'the gravest doubt that the power to dismiss may properly be exercised solely to procure a forced dissolution'.

In the document in which he gave his reasons Kerr didn't refer to this advice from the law officers. He simply asserted the opposite. It was only because the law officers' advice was later leaked to the *Australian Financial Review* that Australians learned that it existed. Kerr did not release it at the same time as he released the statement by Chief Justice Barwick. We don't know whether Kerr revealed to Barwick that the law officers' advice existed when he asked Barwick's opinion. Even more curious is that Kerr said he would be surprised if the law officers of the Crown would doubt his reserve power to do what he did. A week before he had read a document from them in which they had questioned using the kinds of action he may already have been contemplating.

It would have been both in the interests of responsible government and within possible meanings of the words of the Constitution that Kerr should have done nothing except follow the government's advice to him. But that doesn't mean that he couldn't put up ideas of his own. A Governor-General can put up ideas which, if his government accepts them, become the government's advice to him. Here is another puzzle in Kerr's actions: from Whitlam's account, Kerr had been taking no real initiatives; he gave the impression he was leaving initiatives to the government. Then suddenly – no warning! – he takes the most politically violent and most controversial action imaginable, short of interpreting his position as Commander-in-Chief literally and calling out the troops.

If he was going to butt in – I don't think he should have, but say he did – he ought to have begun very low key, looking for ways of avoiding accusations of partisanship, going for the solution that was least disturbing. Instead he abruptly took an action that made more disturbance than any other possible decision. Perhaps he simply didn't understand his job. He may have seen himself up on the bench, handing down a judgment, written up strongly, as is the lawyer's way, in order to sound better than any other argument. (Although judges often at least acknowledge the existence of other arguments.) Then to get rid of Whitlam and put in Fraser, he became the court's sheriff, executing the judge's order. Judges don't say what is in their minds. They don't use the methods of discussion, diplomacy, compromise. They secretly decide what they will do. Then they do it.

Numbers of people have discussed one particular type of action Kerr might have taken, either 'on advice' (that is, suggesting to the government they suggest it to him) or off his own bat (in which case he would have had to do it very softly). This was that, in one of several ways, he could have directly approached the Senate. He might have suggested that it might not be constitutional to defer supply until the government called an election: that they should either accept the money Bills or reject them, but not defer them on a condition. Faced with this, some Senators may have refused to reject the Bills. The crisis would have been over. Or he might have indicated that he was taking the Senate's deferral as a rejection, and therefore the first leg of the three month process necessary for a double dissolution: that also might have secured the passing of the Bills. Or he might have expressed doubts as to the constitutionality of the Senate rejecting money Bills.

In the lawyer's way, in his own statement he strongly ruled out other possibilities: he didn't refer to the Constitution's provision of a double dissolution as the way out of a deadlock. He preferred his own style of intervention as 'the only solution'. And of the Senate's powers he said 'the Senate undoubtedly has constitutional power to refuse or defer supply to the government'. The 'undoubtedly' is nonsense. The two principal law officers of the crown had advised him a week before that the Senate had no express constitutional authority to impose conditions before dealing with money Bills. Even the Chief Justice, although he said the Senate had the constitutional power to refuse a money Bill, did not specifically say it had the power to defer such Bills. There was doubt even on the matter of its power to reject. Several authorities suggested the Senate did not have the right to reject money Bills. (The clause expressly giving the Senate this power was deleted from the drafts of the Constitution.) One of these authorities was Sir Richard Eggleston, a retired judge who was also on Whitlam's short list for Governor-General.

Perhaps the most unpleasant of all the curious aspects of Kerr's action is that Whitlam says that at no time did Kerr give any indication that he was considering dismissal of the government. If this is true, it was inefficient as well as deceitful for Kerr not to tell Whitlam he was contemplating dismissing him. It is not to the point to say, as Kerr did in his statement, that Whitlam would not change his mind. He could have tried him out. If he had been ready to dismiss Whitlam from the beginning of the crisis, he should have told Whitlam so; Whitlam would then have had the chance of calling a half-Senate election or of giving some other advice. If Kerr changed his mind in the course of the crisis, he gave a false impression by not telling Whitlam that he was now considering his dismissal. Perhaps he did tell Whitlam what was in his mind, but Whitlam didn't understand it. But if he did not speak frankly to Whitlam of what was in his mind, while this would have been proper in a judge, it was most improper in a Governor-General.

Some of Kerr's supporters are now spreading the story that he maintained secrecy because otherwise Whitlam might have advised Queen Elizabeth to dismiss him, and that would have 'involved the Crown'. Irrespective of whether this touched on Kerr's motives, or whether Whitlam would have taken such an action, it seems worth noting that (a) Kerr involved the Crown anyway by his own action, except that in its effects his action favoured the Opposition rather than the government and (b) the convention of responsible government is that the Crown should take the advice of its ministers.

Eleven years before the 1975 election my book *The Lucky Country* was published and it included a reference to the need for Australia to become a republic. At the time leftover royalists treated this as treason; most of the kind of people I was more likely to know treated it as an amusing eccentricity. What did it matter if Australia was still in theory a monarchy? The Governor-General was only a harmless figurehead. There were more important matters to worry about.

Now we have a position in which apparently the Senate is virtually of equal power to the House of Representatives, so that to govern confidently a party must have a majority in both Houses. The Prime Minister and most of the ministry still sit in the House of Representatives, but there is nothing in the Constitution that would prevent the whole of the ministry sitting in the Senate. To match this uncertainty in Parliament House, there is a new uncertainty about Government House: a Governor-General is now assumed to have such of the reserve powers of King George III as he cares to exercise.

It would be essential in a democratic Constitution for the Senate to lose all legislative powers and perhaps be abolished. A democratic constitution would state that the House of Representatives alone could choose the Prime Minister, or sack him. As far as possible the head of state should be stripped of power. For example, the Executive Council should disappear, the control of the armed services by the elected government should be precisely stated and it should be clear that High Court judges are elected by Parliament.

At present Australia is, in ceremonial terms, a monarchy. In effective political terms it is not a monarchy, but a governor-generalate. Queen Elizabeth made it clear, in her letter to the Speaker of the House of Representatives, that the government of Australia is not her precinct. Australia should be changed by referendum from a governor-generalate to a republic. (The word 'Commonwealth' can be kept: it can be taken to mean republic.) The head of state of the Commonwealth of Australia, mainly a ceremonial figure, should be elected as the President of West Germany is – by majority vote, without debate, in a Federal Convention consisting of the members of the House of Representatives and an equal number of members elected by the Lower Houses of the State Parliaments according to the principle of proportional representation. The head of state could be called President, or if that sounds too fancy, Head of State. I would once have said that, for old times' sake we might have kept 'Governor-General' as the Americans kept 'Governor'. After John Kerr's action I don't think that any more.

Six
The Hoax of the Economic Crisis

It was at the beginning of the Senate crisis. The politicians who controlled the 'States' House' were told by their parties to block the government's money Bills. They obeyed. My wife and I were at the Lakeside Hotel in Canberra, for the Metal Trades Industries Association annual meeting, at which I was one of the speakers. When the MTIA delegates had arrived the night before some had been perplexed by what Fraser was doing, but Liberal Party shadow ministers began moving amongst them, in the politician's manner casting up simple shapes to explain complex events, and by the lunchtime speeches the next day everything seemed to be coming together.

At the evening banquet, Jim McClelland was there for the government and Malcolm Fraser for the Opposition. Fraser was still nervously crumbling and nibbling toast melba after eating smoked salmon, mushroom soup, veal in a piquant sauce, pudding, and choice of cheese. The toast melba suddenly reminded me of Sydney University Union Night Debates Dinners; I kept on feeling that somehow this *was* a debates dinner. Here we were in our black ties, meeting together in the gentlemanly standards of the after-dinner speech. Manner was more important than substance. We were all students again, practising for when we would become managing directors or Cabinet ministers.

There was another unreality. We belonged to a nation where there was the grand illusion that the economic crisis of combined unemployment and inflation was caused entirely by Gough Whitlam. McClelland pointed out that there was a world crisis of which Australia's experience was only a part but when Fraser presented this as buck-passing there were rustles of assent. When he said surely Australia could find its own answers to economic problems, there was a great cheer.

In the whole history of Australian parochialism I can't recall anything to match the provincial-minded approach to the world economic crisis that marked so many Australians in the years 1973 to 1975. It was extremely convenient for the Liberal Party: without it, Fraser might have lost the election. There seemed to be a genuine belief that somehow, yes, Australia was *the* lucky country, able to go its own way despite what was happening in the rest of the world. There was a refusal to recognize that the capitalist world – the world of the liberal-democratic mixed economies – is going through an economic crisis *from which it may never recover* (in the sense that it may never be the same world again – there will be different rules). Yet, since Australia *is* part of that world, Australian economic life in the future may be unimaginably different. The idea of a return to the old ways might be a dangerous fantasy.

Challenged by this parochialism, throughout last year I tried various devices to point out that there was a *world* economic crisis and that Australia's position was not solely the doing of E. G. Whitlam. Most of these devices didn't work.

One was to try to challenge the habit of selecting unfavourable Australian statistics for comparison with other countries. This was a complete failure. The sharp and concrete presence of some remembered statistic was unassailable. Often the remembered statistic was false. Usually it was a belief in a 20% annual Australian inflation rate. In fact the rate had never been so high but there was no shaking the belief.

The arguments that the 'dole bludgers' had done it, or uniquely high taxation had done it, or Whitlam's welfare state had done it were just as unassailable. Dole bludgers? But, I would say, the Germans pay their unemployed 68% of previous income. High taxation? But, I would say, Australia, taking into account indirect taxation, is one of the least taxed of the prosperous countries; we pay fewer taxes than they do in the United States. Whitlam's welfare state? But, I would say, Australia doesn't rank very high as a welfare state; anyway Sweden, the archetype welfare state (50% taxation compared with 31% in Australia), has one of the lowest inflation rates. Disbelief.

For many people the *but-we-don't-import-oil* syndrome was the clincher. World inflation was caused by the rise in oil prices: Australia doesn't import oil: therefore . . . But, I would say, world inflation was *not* caused by the rise in oil prices. That was only one thing amongst a lot of others. And although we don't import much oil, we do import goods from countries where costs have gone up because the cost of oil has gone up. Some would acknowledge this last point. But to many the oil argument was so self-evident that they wouldn't notice what I was saying.

Many people even jibbed at the idea that our inflation was at least partly related to the costs of imports and exports. At other times it wouldn't have taken long to convince someone that the world commodities price boom of 1972-3 had something to do with Australia's inflation; or that the fact that import prices had gone up by 37% in the twelve months to March 1975 had something to do with Australia's inflation. But this wasn't a normal time. It was a time when people went mad. Even to the extent of not admitting that the world recession had affected the market for some Australian exports.

Try to see Australia in context. The overall look of the world of the affluent countries has been this: in the great boom that started in 1948 they all went through a period of unparalleled confidence in consumer spending, with lavish government spending as well, easy money all round and a combination of technological progress with an endless supply of unskilled labour. In 1960 world liquidity was $70 billion. By 1973 it was $300 billion. There was a general period of 'stagflation' in the capitalist world in the early 1970s. Australia shared it. There was a new boom, 1972-3. Australia shared it. Then a recession hit all these countries. Australia shared that recession. In 1974 there was no economic growth in most of these countries. There was none in Australia. They all suffered business collapses. So did Australia. They knew both unemployment and inflation. So did Australia. There were big government deficits and high interest rates in all these countries, as in Australia. Consumer savings increased rather than consumer demand, as in Australia. In all of them wages went up at the expense of profits and there was loss of business confidence. This also happened in Australia. What in Australia was blamed on to Gough Whitlam's 'socialism', has been a general condition throughout the world of the liberal-democratic mixed-economy countries.

The real economic crisis is that in all prosperous nations, people can no longer be confident that they know what happens in their economies. Inflation in particular seems to have developed mysteries that weren't allowed for. In all these nations, Australia included, the policies that marked the great days of affluence are no longer working. In the affluent days experts imagined that an economy could be controlled by 'fine tuning'. They would keep an eye on the indicators and then make small adjustments in banking and taxation policies, government spending, exchange rates. Now, when these policies are tried, things don't work. A great economic faith has collapsed. As yet, nothing has taken its place. That is why some people, including me, preferred the scepticism and caution of Bill Hayden's approach in 1975 to what seemed the rash romantic belief of Fraser and Lynch that they could gallop back to simple economic verities. Hayden seemed a pragmatist; they seemed dogmatists.

What was it that was so unforgivably bad in Labor's economic performance? I think the greatest mistakes were blunders in political cosmetics, not in economic policy. After they were let out of their cages by the 1972 election the Labor ministers ran off after progress in so many different directions that they didn't seem to notice what the voters could already see every day in the supermarkets: prices were going up. They didn't appear to care about inflation. Whitlam should have put on the kind of theatrical performances staged by the political leaders of most other affluent nations – call national conferences, coin phrases and slogans, produce plans, command the headlines by staged events. This mightn't have done much good for the economy but it could have done a lot of good for the programmes of reform of the Whitlam government. Whitlam need not have sacrificed his programmes; he might have re-examined some of them and translated them into terms of new economic realities, but if he had sold them harder in a context of economic crisis he could have justified keeping most of them. One example: this was the period of advance in equal pay for women. Should that have been abandoned?

As it was, the Opposition were given the chance to pre-empt economic management as a field that was theirs by right and to benefit from the hoax that Australia was not part of the world. When Bill Hayden took over as Treasurer the government began to regain some of its ground. Hayden and McClelland in the Department of Labor were pleasing the media commentators and Wriedt was about to please them as Minister for Minerals and Energy. In a few months the voters might have shared this attitude. It was then – and partly, I believe, for that reason – that the Opposition decided it must force an election.

The main Labor 'blunders' were much the same as blunders made in other countries. Slowness in reaction to the 1972-3 boom ('pace setter' wage claims, the big spending Budget); then over-reaction (the Treasury's tight-money policy became a stranglehold); then over-reaction to the over-reaction (the 'Dr Yes' period of Jim Cairns's Treasurership, when money was poured out to 'the private sector' and in transfer payments to try to keep things going). I wonder what the Liberals' blunders would have been. If McMahon had won the 1972 election, having already increased the money supply and produced an inflationary Budget in 1972, and having kept the exchange rate too low, the Liberals would probably have brought up a disinflationary Budget in 1973. The results would have produced such a panic in 1974 that they would probably have pumped out money as fast as Labor did. And if Snedden had won the 1974 election? Many Labor people now wish he had.

I don't want to make too much of this. Perhaps the Liberals would have been better at controlling inflation than Labor, although under any government our arbitration system might have magnified wage rises as much as it did under Labor. It's possible that the arbitration system, not Labor policies, was the main reason for the high jump of Australian inflation. Even if that is not so, under the Liberals there would still have been an economic crisis. All I am trying to do is to put Labor's performance into perspective. There should have been more media commentators who pointed out (a) that at this time of economic crisis when traditional concepts about economics are no longer working and when traditional policies are producing funny answers everywhere, governments all over the world are getting into varying kinds of messes and (b) the Whitlam government had achievements in economic management as well as blunders. For example, wage indexation (essential, given Australia's arbitration system) and upvaluations of exchange rate (also essential at the commodity boom stage) might not have been carried out so quickly and so well by the Liberals. They might not have been carried out at all. For that matter, even if the Treasury's tight money policy produced difficulties, it was associated with a steadying, then a reduction in the inflation rate.

Even in public clowning and disunity – I wouldn't have been surprised if a Snedden government or a McMahon government had had that, too; although probably no single fiasco would have matched the Khemlani loans affair, an incident that, in itself, had no economic consequences but did make the government seem remarkably stupid. In fact there seemed to be some magic about Khemlani that brought out the farce in whoever touched him. When the Liberals took up with him, they also began to turn themselves into comedians.

In one whole area of industry – farming – where it was most obvious that difficulties were related to world markets rather than Canberra policies (the drop in beef prices, for example), the government was attacked mainly because it was a *Labor* government. However an early impulse by the government to insult farmers had got their backs up. In the same way the Labor government seemed at times out to irritate businessmen – especially miners and manufacturers – to no purpose. No policy was involved; it was just a question of attitude. However it is worth remembering that some of the biggest complaints from farmers and businessmen were not on questions of the private sector getting on with the job under free enterprise market conditions, but of the private sector wanting special help from the government with subsidies, tariffs and other devices that would have to be paid for finally by ordinary Australians.

It's not unusual for politicians to twist around the presentation of a situation to suit themselves, looking for advantage in everything, but there are two great worries about the ease with which the coalition parties and some of the media people were able to build up a picture of uniquely bad economic management and blot out the general world economic crisis. One is that most Australians were left dangerously innocent about how difficult the economic situation was. They could still think there were easy answers, that it was simple to know what was happening, that there were obvious remedies, and that it was just Labor's 'socialism' that stopped it from doing what was needed. The Liberal and National Country Party campaigns aroused in some of the people who voted for them an apocalyptic sense of expectation. Instead of simply coming into power as down-to-earth people who could manage things a bit better, for some voters they became knights in shining armour fighting for the true faith of free enterprise. The other great worry is that some of the Liberal and National Country Party Ministers may themselves believe the nonsense they were pushing during the election.

Several years ago who would have expected a revival of the issue of free enterprise versus socialism? It was a creed that had served the non-Labor parties well since the 1906 election. It had been of memorable importance in the 1949 election. By the late 1960s it seemed dead. Australia had reached a period close to consensus in economic management: in a mixed economy where there was recognition of the importance of both government and business activity, there were only marginal differences between the political parties about how governments should intervene. When I challenged the meeting of North Shore Liberals to produce examples of the 'socialization' they were talking about, all they offered were Medibank and insurance. The first goes back in history to Bismarck's Germany. The second was a proposal (not implemented) to set up a government insurance office to compete with, not to take over from, the private companies. Even the great increase in government expenditure was not 'socialism' – a large part of it was going to State governments and local councils run by non-Labor people. But there was no point in arguing. Reason and consensus had gone. Whitlam equalled 'socialism'.

The old dogma revived because among dormant Liberal beliefs it was a useful kind of explain-all, and the crisis of inflation demanded explanation. World inflation is not only an economic crisis. It is a cultural crisis and in such a crisis there can be a return to the consolations of old faiths. A large part of Australians' values are measured in money. Describe our economic life and you describe a large part of our culture. Even those (most Australians) for whom inflation meant continuing prosperity could feel a kind of culture shock when the sense of value in money declined so quickly. A significant proportion of them reactivated old beliefs; a desire to go back to the past is a natural reaction to challenge. But it doesn't work.

Seven
Vendetta Journalism

As a young journalist in 1949 I wrote a satirical series, 'The Golden Age', that made fun of the Chifley government every Saturday in the Sydney *Daily Telegraph*. As a middle-aged editor in 1968 I was the first political critic to question John Gorton's capability, with an article in the *Bulletin*. 'Is he John the Bold, or Gorton the Unready?' I've known the thrill of the chase in trying to kill governments. But what occurred to me during the 1975 election, as it did to practising journalists who were shouldered out of the way in their own newspapers to make way for other views, was the potential political evil when, in effect, all the main newspapers are enjoying the thrill of the chase *in the one direction*.

On my way to the eye doctor on the third day of the election campaign, I tested my sight by using one of the afternoon newspaper posters as an eye chart. GOUGH PANICS: CHEAP RENTS, but in the first edition the heading on the story had read merely: GOUGH'S PROMISE: CHEAP RENTS. Each day in hospital I asked my wife what the posters were saying and as she and other visitors read me newspaper headings and snatches of editorials, I felt for the first time in my life a kind of shame for having been a journalist. Two foreign journalists who came to see me in hospital said they felt it too. The unanimous stridency of the newspaper vendetta was for them a uniquely Australian characteristic of the election. All my life I have defended the right of newspapers to say what they like. I would make qualifications now.

I know that research has suggested that interpersonal relations may be more important in how people vote than direct newspaper influence, and that newspapers' main influence may be confirming views already held, and I'm aware that newspapers produce results different from those intended. A friend of mine was undecided on how to vote until she read the *Sydney Morning Herald* editorial on December 12: ('The monument to three years of socialist rule is plain to see: a confident and prosperous country reduced to uncertainty and recession, with a record rate of inflation and record unemployment, with high taxes and high prices, with thousands of businesses ruined and commerce stagnating, with a rural sector facing disaster.') That ended her indecision. She voted Labor. But we can't afford to assume that media conduct is not important in political life. Research into media influence has been extremely limited. Between elections the media provide the basic day-to-day information about what is supposed to be happening and what is supposed to matter in politics and in the world generally. They play a large part in maintaining the sense of drama that can be so important in politics. In an election itself they may appear to set the official agenda. Sometimes – as in the 1975 election – they can become more visible campaigners than the leaders themselves.

What appears in the media can also have a direct effect on politicians. They are part of the inside game. The *Australian* and the *Daily Telegraph* were using the phrase 'election fever' well before general talk of an election; the use of this phrase may have been part of establishing the mood which produced the election. When Malcolm Fraser announced he intended to use the Senate to dismiss the government a gambit of his was that newspaper editorials had all called him to the helm; later in the week the Liberal Party took an ad quoting bits of these editorials. It was newspapers that created the Khemlani loans affair; they put it on a plate for the Liberals; the Liberals' own contributions were so incompetent that they were beginning to discredit them.

Seen like this, the media prove a more important part of our political system than are many activities (for instance, parliamentary debates) acknowledged as political. Yet, except for the ABC, all the media are owned by profit-seeking companies. So we have a problem: profit-seeking companies own a highly significant part of the Australian political system. What other parts of our political system are owned by profit-seeking companies?

Saying that people who control the media have the right to say what they like was an appropriate view in the eighteenth-century days of a multiplicity of small journals and pamphlets putting forward diverse views, and no mass circulation newspapers. Now we have big audiences and oligopolic control. It is not just a question of the rights of media-controllers; it is also a question of what conduct should prevail in an important part of the Australian political system. Why should we tolerate a situation in which the bias in all the media by accident or design can favour one party?

The Whitlam government will be treated by historians as one of the great governments in Australia's history. Yet, from day to day the media increasingly presented it as a government of crooks and clowns. It helped redefine Australia in the world, giving it that more independent look Dr Evatt had attempted to move towards in the 1940s. Australia could begin to seem something more than the southern agent of the rich white nations of the north. The Whitlam government redefined Australia's attitudes towards export of its resources, with more emphasis on Australia's interests and less emphasis on the interests of its rich foreign customers. By destroying, at least in token form, what was left of the White Australia Policy and by making some Third World noises, the government began to move against outside prejudices towards Australia. By certain changes in national symbols and national styles, and by the encouragement of the arts, it assisted the development of a more confident national consciousness. It moved against injustice towards women, Aborigines, immigrants, and other disadvantaged groups. It made access to legal advice less dependent on wealth. It presided over a more tolerant Australia, among other things further relaxing censorship and the divorce laws. In a great number of ways it moved Australian approaches to welfare closer to those of the prosperous Western European countries. In a general shift in spending policy it produced a concept of Australia as an educated and predominantly urban society. It almost completely modernized the Australian political agenda.

In making that summary I have deliberately put up the most favourable picture I could manage. I think that is the kind of emphasis historians, looking for achievement, will make. What made the biggest headlines will often seem too minor to record.

Why didn't these achievements come through more strongly in the media? For some of the media controllers a lot of the changes were not reforms at all, but reprehensible radicalism. And by 1975 other media, particularly the Sydney afternoon newspapers and the Murdoch papers, seemed simply in for the kill. There is also a more general explanation: we all tend to trivialize experience into matters of simple personality and anecdote; to do this is a natural media characteristic. Given this, in order to interest voters an effective politician would trivialize political programmes. But the Whitlam government sadly lacked this sort of effective politician. It was more remarkable for egocentric muck-ups.

Even so, why didn't the media do a better reporting job? Many journalists, including many whose bias was towards Labor, were not able to work out how to report a reform government. Most journalists had no memories of such a government. Traditions of making interesting news out of policies had atrophied from lack of use. In addition, the buffooneries of Liberal governments in decline had already trivialized politics beyond ordinary measure. For most younger political journalists this was the main style they knew.

Techniques developed during the Liberals' silly season were soon applied to the Whitlam government. From the ASIO affair to the Morosi affair, the stories most confidently handled were exemplifications of silliness.

The silly season phase ran almost by itself up to the 1974 election and overlapped the next phase – that of misreporting the economic crisis. In the final debauch of the election campaign this misreporting in some cases became either gross incompetence or deliberate misrepresentation. But the great reporting crimes, of which, in varying degrees, almost all newspapers were guilty, were failing to report Australia's economic problems in the context of a world economic crisis, and failing to consistently report the world economic crisis itself. In some cases this may simply have been due to lack of flair, or an inability to see the wood for the trees. In some it may have been deliberate misrepresentation. In others it may have been a simple faith that Australia was not part of the world. Whatever the motive, if there was one way in which almost all the media came together to destroy the government unfairly, it was this.

Just go back to that December 12 *Sydney Morning Herald* editorial. Notice that it says the rural sector was facing disaster. In itself this is nonsense. Disaster does not usually face all Australian farmers, only different types of farmers at different times. But its implication is that farmers' difficulties were the fault of the Whitlam government. Yet most rural difficulties would have been exactly the same under any other government. Because they came from slumps in world markets, not the Whitlam government.

The third phase – the Khemlani loans fiasco – was overlapped by the first two and had elements of each. The newspapers that did most to break this story did so with professional standards of journalism. They made public matters that should never have been secret, even if at times the technique of the huge headline and the photostat became an addiction not always justified by what was in the photostat. But too much was made out of the story; there were many important matters of public policy in Australia other than the government's silly dealings with Khemlani. And there were innuendoes of personal corruption for which there was absolutely no evidence; what the evidence suggested was improper secrecy and remarkable silliness. Both publicly and in a particularly unscrupulous whisper campaign the Liberals tried to change the aspect from one of folly to one of personal corruption and some of this got through to the voters, who saw the government as dishonest, although there was no evidence of this.

The last phase was the election period itself, although this for some newspapers had begun well before, as a campaign to force an election. During the election, four of the Sydney newspapers, the *Sun*, the *Australian*, the *Daily Mirror* and the *Daily Telegraph* went after the Labor Party with techniques no newspaper has used within my adult lifetime, but to condemn these four newspapers is not to praise the others. For instance the *Sydney Morning Herald* in its news pages was following traditional standards of fairness and all credit to it, but these standards can include anomalies. To take one example: its main front page story on December 11 was P.M. STRUCK BY BEER CAN. On December 13 in the course of a story on page seven, if you read far enough down, you could have learned that someone threw a soft drink can at Whitlam, but missed. Is this huge difference between a main heading on page one, and an obscure paragraph on page seven, due to the fact that one thrower of cans was a better shot than the other? Or was a beer can thrown at Fraser more newsy than a soft drink can thrown at Whitlam?

One of my main concerns in hospital was to cheer everybody up. Footsteps would come into my room; according to whomever the owner of the footsteps was proclaimed to be - nurse, sister, visitor, cleaner, trolley man, pharmacist, doctor, Red Cross lady - I would try some cheering message: *I feel fine ... yes, I like the food ... what cassette would you like to hear? ... no, I haven't got a headache ... have a chocolate ... yes, I can do it myself ...* and when it was time to change my dressing: *I can see two fingers ... four fingers.* To begin with, I would try to cheer visiting Labor voters by saying that Fraser's economic policy wouldn't stand up to questioning. But in the last week I stopped saying this. His economic policy was standing up. Because it wasn't being seriously questioned. Fraser's tactic was not to answer questions. And he got away with it. By these means, in a particularly important respect, the media played it Fraser's way.

Normally the media simply hammer at an election campaigner who seems to be promising a lot. They ask, over and over again, one question: *but where will you find the money?* If he doesn't answer, they expose him. Fraser's tactic worked only because the media didn't expose his evasiveness. How was it that in this campaign one of the most commonplace devices of media questioning was not adequately used? One might add another question: why was Fraser's diversionary tactic of false 'revelations' not adequately exposed?

What made him safe in his campaign style of diversion and evasion was that in this election journalist-commentators prominent in elections since 1969 were sat on. When newspaper managements announce that they will report without bias, reserving comment to their editorials, this may mean they want to shut up journalist-commentators and run only the comments the management wants to run. In the degrading election of 1975 this meant that routine methods of exposure of evasion and diversion were not used, or were used inadequately. If covering the election had been left to the journalists they would have brought Fraser out into the open, changed the nature of his campaign and given the voters a better chance to know what was happening. And they would have done this not from bias, but by using routine techniques.

Even if ordinary standards of competence and something

higher than minimum standards of fairness had been followed, and there had not been all those vindictive, triumphant headlines turning whole newspapers into sneering pamphlets, there would still have remained the unseemliness that comes when every mass-circulation publication in the country and almost every one of the smaller publications is publishing editorials against one party and in favour of another.

I hate newspaper editorials. When I went back to editing the *Bulletin* in 1967, my first change was to cut out editorials. An editorial has the mystification of anonymity and group identity. Yet this is just a hoax. It is written by one person (perhaps altered by others) either expressing his own views, or views he has been told to express, or views that have come as a compromise out of a meeting between several people. That is all it is. It gives itself the authority and magic of an anonymous group identity – set in special type, and often expressed in a special kind of bombast not otherwise seen in the publication it appears in – but it is just some stuff someone wrote. It is not 'the paper's opinion'. It may express opinions opposite to those of people who work for the publication. Most of them may despise it.

People have to get along with reading a daily newspaper, making friendly compromises, yet this great blaring self-important thing, the editorial, tries to speak in their name. Sometimes it swells in size; sometimes it jumps into the front page, declaring itself more important than the news. At the end of the campaign the editorials in the *Age* were so unfriendly to at least one of its readers that she wrote to me from Melbourne to say that for two days running they had made her cry.

In the interests of greater seemliness in elections I would like a law ensuring that every election article in a newspaper or magazine was signed by its author. That would do away with the fake authority of editorials. Editorials would simply be articles with someone's name on them. Signing articles might also provide some kind of check on the secret re-writing of stories alleged to have happened in several newspapers in the 1975 election. And – if supported by other actions – it would be commensurate with the only way out of the scandal of an important part of the political system appearing so biased: the provision of a variety of interpretations in each newspaper; of these a management line would be merely one amongst many.

I think I would leave direct government intervention at that: all election articles to be signed by the author. This is not to say a government couldn't experiment more generally in a variety of ways to encourage greater diversity in print media. But reform of the existing media will be most effective if it comes from within the media itself.

When I was a university student I saw myself as a syndicalist – let the producers band together and run their own activities. It was a rather abstract matter. There didn't seem any prospect of anything happening. But in the Eye Hospital, when I heard on the radio that journalists on the *Australian* and the *Daily Telegraph* had gone on strike in protest against what was being done on those two papers I heard myself cheer out loud. In Australian newspapers there had never been such a principled strike before. The producers were concerned with the principles of their craft.

The media will change if journalists, imbued with a general spirit, keeping a sense of openness and co-operation, bring pressure where they work to maintain standards of professional responsibility. This is a task that has already been taken up by some editors; they risk their jobs in tensions with management and sometimes lose them. At the *Australian*, the staff felt helpless, professionally degraded: the main political stories were being put together secretly by executives on the back bench. Arbitrariness and conspiracy can be removed from media offices if journalists don't allow them.

This strike was one of the heartening signs of new consciousness emerging in this election from a recognition of injustice and defeat. If journalists can maintain that vision – and they are only likely to do so as a group – they should not seek perfection. Merely remedying obvious evil will do. Their objective should be this: there is no commercial reason why newspapers, as profit-seeking organizations, have to campaign in elections. So let them stop doing so. Why should their managements enjoy such an extraordinary privilege in our political system, that it gives them a more assured position during an election than even the leaders of the major political parties? In elections journalists should set an ideal. Perhaps it can't be reached, but it could lead to improvement. It should be that a daily newspaper provides a comprehensive reporting service on the election and a variety of interpretative opinions, but it does not itself appear to campaign.

Eight
The Return of the Has-Beens?

I had never before worn a political badge – 'Independence for Australia', it said, with the Eureka flag on it. The occasion was a 'People for Whitlam' dinner party to raise campaign money at Harry and Penelope Seidler's house at Killara on Sydney's North Shore, and it seemed to demand a conversation piece. As it turned out most people didn't recognize the Eureka flag and, anyway, the conversation piece was being there. It was a coming-out occasion, a declaration. It was also a very good party.

Outside, on the footpath, there was a picket of a few of the embattled North Shore bourgeoisie, their children and their dogs. There we were, inside the Seidlers' contemporary palace, drinking champagne, and using big words: outside were simple, bare-footed Liberal voters, threatened by rain. The Whitlams arrived. The picketing Liberals booed, then sang 'God Save the Queen'. When the Whitlams came inside we clapped, and those who could remember the words sang 'Advance Australia Fair'. Later in the evening someone said in a patronizing aristocratic way how good it was to see those middle-class people outside taking an interest in politics.

But if their interest in politics was accurately represented by the song they sang, it was an interest in the politics of the past, just as at the North Shore Liberal Party meeting I had addressed earlier in the week the fanatical revival of free enterprise dogma represented a return to the politics of the past. This was to be one of the great concerns after the election: had the voters put into power a government of has-beens unable to react to contemporary circumstances?

It was partly a question of whether Fraser would steady

down now that he had the job, and be careful not to offend any more of the tenuous traditions of democratic government, or whether the 'revelations', evasions and 1949 rhetoric of the election campaign were his natural style. It was partly fear of authoritarianism. Were we in for a period of union bashing? Would the hardliners in his government suppress some of the new freedoms of the 1970s? One of the spectres at the 'People for Whitlam' feast had been the possibility of the massacre of the ABC rock station 2JJ and the radio programme *Lateline*. One of the Asian staff of the Eye Hospital feared a return to the 'whites only' policy (a policy which would leave the hospital somewhat understaffed). But the most basic question was: whether or not they moved to right-wing excesses, did the Liberals know enough about the mid-1970s to run a government? Or would they be troublemakers who created disorder because they couldn't understand change? It had been said in criticism when Don Chipp was a minister in 1972 that he was 'attuned to the twentieth century'. After the election we found that Chipp was not a minister.

For many of those most attentive to politics, what gave Whitlam his appeal in 1972 was his sense of contemporaneity. He was not resisting the times. He was trying to understand them. The attitudes and priorities that Whitlam dramatized were already spread out among the community and in theory most might equally well have been taken up by a non-Labor party. The 1971-4 phenomenon of the Liberal 'trendies' showed that some of them were trying to do this, but it was Whitlam who defined new realities, expressed new values and seemed to reach out for the new, creative moods of the age. That he didn't meet all expectations is not surprising. Politicians never do. But he did redefine what Australian poltics might be about.

People forced towards the Labor Party by the conduct of the Liberals in their shabby frenetic stage had imagined that, after Whitlam's win in 1972, the Liberals would refurbish and come out fighting the 1975 election looking like a contemporary political party. They came out looking like 1949.

That may merely have been opportunism. If this is so, the first people to be disappointed will be the singers of 'God Save the Queen' and the chanters of the litanies of free enterprise. This morning I saw in the *Sydney Morning Herald* a letter saying that if the Fraser government didn't keep its promise to abolish the Prices Justification Tribunal 'they deserve to be voted out at the first opportunity', as people who lacked integrity. Perhaps they will make token changes, as they did before Christmas, when they sweated over a few minor economies, then spent what they saved re-instituting the school cadets; then they could more or less go on where Labor left off, but more slowly, consolidating, giving people a rest from politics. But during the election there were promises to turn Labor's world upside down (and part of the world of Menzies as well). Some of the Liberals' more ambitious promises ('the most far-sighted since Federation' said Fraser) for smaller government and greater federalism could be more radical changes than anything attempted by Whitlam. In his compulsive centralism Whitlam was simply amplifying existing trends.

In either the case of giving people a rest from politics or of trying to turn Labor's world upside down (note that the two promises contradict each other), there is an assumption that Australia will stay still while all this happens. But the late 1970s won't stand still. They will be a time of changes that will challenge the two strongest beliefs of the Liberals – the belief in the primacy of economic development and 'free enterprise', and the belief in Australia as a branch office of rich white nations in the northern hemisphere.

The belief in the primacy of economic development and 'free enterprise' faces five challenges:

The challenge of 'corporatism'. Half the goods made in Australia are manufactured by only 200 firms. The shopkeepers' ethic of the free market and of 'individualism' may still apply to small firms and some professional people but it is challenged by the increasing importance of big business. Now that the apparatus of economic management by 'fine tuning' seems to be falling apart throughout the affluent world we may be entering a 'corporatist' stage of capitalism in which more things will be arranged in direct dealing between three types of big corporations – big business, big unions and big government agencies. Does this simply mean that more of the affairs of Australia will be run directly by 200 or so big firms, most of them foreign? If not what checks are there? The first check is that the big firms themselves should be forced into profit-sharing schemes and schemes for employees to participate in management. In addition, Australia's 300 or so unions might amalgamate into a couple of dozen big ones for better bargaining. But if that happens shouldn't they also be forced into ensuring greater internal democracy? And a lot would be demanded of government agencies. They would have to make a large number of value judgements, set a lot of guidelines, develop a high degree of technocracy. Yet aren't there also dangers there?

The challenge of participation. Even if big business, big unions and big governments are checked by participatory devices there would still be a need for more community action. Some of the forms for community action have already developed. Just before I started writing this chapter I heard on the radio news that seventy local organizations have come together to form the Botany Bay Action Committee to fight plans to make Botany Bay a major port: resident action committees, consumer groups and so forth may more and more become regular features of administration. As I am writing now I am listening to 2MBS-FM, Sydney's co-operative FM station: the co-operative is also becoming one of our new organizational styles.

At the other end of the radio band is 2JJ and in between there is an ethnic radio station: government agencies have begun to provide access facilities (for a wide range of activities) over which they exercise little control.

The challenge of unemployment. The great affluent era of full employment may now be finished. We may have lost the trick of providing employment for everyone, without inflation. We may have to abandon the idea that people can have the right to economic dignity only if they have 'jobs'. If full employment goes we will have to find means of attaching dignity to 'dole-bludging'. One way out is to define 'work' differently, so that it goes beyond matters connected with buying and selling; for example, why are women who run houses and rear children not seen as productive by our economic system?

The challenge of manufacturing. Throughout the Menzies era the growth of manufacturing was seen as the great key to continuing human progress. The factory was the symbol of what mattered. Now it isn't. It was part of Whitlam's sense of the present that he understood the new importance of services, such as urban amenities, education, leisure pursuits, and, in his 25% cut in tariffs, that he was sceptical about the necessary goodness of all manufacturing. Manufacturing is losing its importance and its dynamic in all affluent societies. Because Australia is such a big exporter of the products of mines and farms, it could be easier for Australia to shift resources away from factories than most other industrial nations. Perhaps this would mean fewer 'jobs', but it could mean more money to go around, and with tariffs lowered and more imports coming cheaply into the country, a lot of what we bought would cost less.

The challenge to 'the economic'. In ways we can't yet accurately describe, the great era of continuing 'growth' and 'development' has produced possibly invincible resistances to its own continued progress. We may be seeing the end of the period when the economic is the main measure of value. Things no longer work as they used to. Perhaps the moods of some of the alternative societies tell us something: more concern with performance for its own sake, more co-operation, greater simplicity and frugality in lifestyles, a seeking for naturalness.

Now, what of the conservative vision of Australia as a successful branch office of northern hemisphere interests? Some conservative Australians have acted like foreign agents of the British, the Americans, or of anti-communism or world capitalism, or of their own view of European culture. They saw Australia's main importance, or its *only* importance, in serving these foreign interests. Others have seen Australia as having separate interests, but have seen these interests secured only in complete involvement with one or more of the northern hemisphere nations. The dangers of this approach have been demonstrated since Singapore fell in 1942. But some of them became more explicit in the Whitlam years.

Australia as a commercial agent for foreigners. Despite flounderings, the Whitlam period began the first thorough reappraisal of the traditional attitude of seeing Australia as a nation so dependent on what it exports that it should give its customers more loyalty than it shows to itself. The first shapes – albeit rather wobbly – were cast up of a world in which there were more ambiguous trading loyalties. Australia as a prosperous industrialized country is an affluent society, part of 'the West', but as an exporter of raw materials it can also see itself associated with Third World countries. As well as this new sense of definition, there continued the questioning, that began with John McEwen and John Gorton, of the part foreign companies should play in Australia.

Australia as a diplomatic agent for foreigners. Whitlam dramatized how Australians could act, or at least appear to act, with greater independence in foreign affairs. They could remain an ally of a great power without displaying colonial subservience. Remember how one of the early Liberal and newspaper campaigns against Whitlam was that he might shame Australia by not being invited to the White House by Richard Nixon?

Australia as a military agent for foreigners. An ingrained view of Australia, institutionalized in Anzac Day, our most effective attempt at a national day, is of an expeditionary power which expresses its loyalty to a great and powerful friend, as well as its most profound moments of national self-definition, by sending troops overseas to be killed in the great friend's wars. This has been, in effect, Australia's 'defence policy'. The idea of basing military planning on any assumption other than that of the faithful little ally was never seriously examined by the conservative political parties. In a proclaimed policy of 'continental defence', Labor began to dismantle this assumption. If almost completely unsuccessfully, it tried – although not very often – to look for a national rather than an interventionary defence policy.

Australia as a cultural agent for foreigners. The development of new national consciousness was in progress long before Gough Whitlam became Prime Minister. But he came to office at a time of greater confidence in the élite arts, popular entertainment, even advertising campaigns. In some way – perhaps from the government money given to the arts – Whitlam became associated with this new self-confidence. In the field of national symbols he was clearly innovative: he was the first Prime Minister to begin dismantling forms proclaiming the 'Britishness', and therefore the lack of a national identity, of Australia; and he removed the last official tokens of Australia's exclusive whiteness.

In the 1969 election a majority of voters wanted Labor, not the coalition partners, to be the government; but the electoral system decided otherwise. John Gorton remained Prime Minister. From this all of Labor's subsequent troubles flowed. If Whitlam had won office in 1969 he would have found no world economic crisis to interrupt the programme of change he had been putting together since the 1950s. By the 1972 election, he could have gone to the people as a great reformer, perhaps already a man of the past, but worth another go. And, since he might have run out of policies by then, as a politician looking for something new he might have welcomed the economic crisis as a way of fashioning new ideas out of new events.

Apart from the outrages committed in campaigns to destroy the Labor government, what was of concern in the 1975 election was that, like Whitlam in 1972, Fraser seemed a man going into the job with fixed ideas, although, unlike Whitlam, he didn't tell us any of the details. Was he likely to fashion new policies in response to new events? The question had special meaning because of the way the problems of the future so challenge the greatest faiths of the Liberal Party. Although its faith in its right to rule could lead to a saving opportunism.

Some of the Labor Party's greatest strength now lies outside the parliamentary party – in the good people defeated in the 1975 elections, and in those who have joined the party, stirred to action by the assault on it, or those who, though not joining it, have come to wish it well. Thrown into exile, can the party draw on the new consciousness of politics of tens of thousands of Australians who saw themselves personally defeated on 13 December 1975? Would it be ridiculous to imagine that party branches and sympathetic independent organizations could play a greater community role? And that the party could find new sources of energy and new approaches to deal with an increasingly strange world?

If the world economic crisis continues it will wash Malcolm Fraser away in the 1978 election and wash Labor back into power. This time Labor must be more ready for power than it was in 1972. Perhaps Labor has one thing going for it. It still has many of its own commitments to the past, God knows, but the perils of office did, with luck, destroy some of them. At least Labor may be less committed than its opponents to the kind of Australia that, I think, may be doomed.

Nine
'Let The People Think'

It was about half past three in the morning when I woke up the day after Bjelke-Petersen had produced his 'revelations' that two of Whitlam's ministers were corrupt, but had given neither the names of the ministers nor details of the alleged corruption.

With the transistor plug in my ear, to a background of 2JJ's rock music and late night chit-chat, sometimes dozing a bit, but then coming back to consciousness, I wrote a small pamphlet in my head. I rehearsed it to myself later while I was fed, washed, shaved and put into clean pyjamas, and then through two news sessions, the *AM* public affairs programme, a Telemann cassette, a Bach cassette and Act 3 of Shakespeare's *Julius Caesar*, also on cassette. After my wife arrived I dictated it to her and asked her to give it to anyone who wanted it.

Like many others during the election, I was involved in actions that in our thin experience of politics in Australia had previously been subjects for fantasy – addressing a rally of 10,000 people, now ready to release a pamphlet to the nation. But it turned out to be only a leaflet, and most of the nation didn't see it. The organization 'Citizens for Democracy' decided that they wanted instead a 'We Accuse' Manifesto; the *National Citizen* didn't print it after all; it was going to be distributed at 'Light a Candle for Democracy', then it wasn't. So far as I know its only use was that 12,000 copies were handed out on North Shore railway stations, 12,000 copies went to homes and shopping centres in the northern beaches area, and 25,000 copies were handed out in Bill McMahon's electorate.

It began: 'Fellow Australians! We are now entering the last

dangerous days of the most sustained and corrupting campaign to destroy a government in our national history ...' After twenty paragraphs, it ended: 'In the stirring days when popular Australian democracy was beginning to form there would sometimes be great processions of ordinary people marching behind a simple slogan which said: BEHOLD THE PEOPLE THINK. God knows what lies may confront the people in the next ten days, but in their hearts people can know right from wrong. Let the people think!' My wife called it: LET THE PEOPLE THINK.

But it is not just a question of whether the people think, it is also what concepts they think with. I would guess there were two types of people highly motivated against John Kerr's action. One included people who identified themselves as Labor supporters, or more generally as 'working class', or who saw themselves as reformers in general or as people concerned with particular issues – welfare, for instance. They had an animal reaction of anger or fear. They knew they were threatened. The other type (some people were both types at once) were those who had certain concepts of democracy – whether precise, or vague. When aspiring democrats carried their banners saying BEHOLD THE PEOPLE THINK, they assumed that it was an essential part of a political system that its framework be taught in schools. That does not necessarily happen in Australia. There may be no other country where less regard is paid in schools to passing on simple ideas about the political system. It is not uncommon in any country for some voters to know little about the political system; what is uncommon is that Australia doesn't really try. Here is a situation that can be described factually as the end of responsible government in Australia, and in a newspaper letter two professors of politics dismiss it as a 'temporary technical difficulty in the working of our parliamentary system'. Understandably it was difficult for the people to do much thinking.

The level of competence in the questioning of Fraser on the

constitutional situation by television and radio interviewers was close to zero. I don't recall one interviewer who seemed to know what 'responsible government' was, so that Fraser was able to get away with talking about 'responsibility to Parliament' as meaning responsibility to both Houses, instead of to the more democratically elected House. The way the question of responsible government was shrugged off by editorial-writers in most newspapers may have been due as much to ignorance as to duplicity.

I don't recall any attempt to get across the point that the Senate's cutting off the government's supply of money was not the same as a vote of no confidence by the House of Representatives. Such cutting off might mean that the government would be finally forced to call an election, but it could possibly do so to its advantage. Instead of fighting an election in which they might have been seen by a significant number of voters as scoundrels dismissed by the Governor-General for inefficiency and crookedness, the Whitlam government could have fought the election on the grounds that the Opposition were scoundrels so hungry for office that they used their majority in the Senate to cut off the people's money, causing hardship and ruin. Marginal irrationalities of this kind can win elections.

At times in a nation's history some significant part of its political culture is challenged: such times can be seen as testing the resilience of the whole society. They can also be seen as a particular test of the nation's culture-bearing élites. What are we to say of a nation in which, when one of the basic conventions of its political system is changed, large sections of its élites do not even know that the change has happened.

For me one of Whitlam's great moments was when he stood on the steps of Parliament House before all of us in front of our television sets while the proclamation dismissing the Parliament was read out by Kerr's secretary, and then said:

'Ladies and gentlemen, well may we say God save the Queen, because nothing will save the Governor-General. The proclamation which you have just heard read was counter-signed by Malcolm Fraser, who will undoubtedly go down in Australia's history, on Remembrance Day, 1975, as Kerr's cur.' I got so excited when I saw this that I spilt my drink: here was the outspokenness of a plain Australian.

Yet many Australians saw this as Whitlam's worst moment: he had been rude to Queen Elizabeth, the Governor-General and the Prime Minister, and he had used an insulting word in public. Not only had he been disloyal, he had not even been respectable.

Their reaction provides two of several answers to the questions: What are thought of as the legitimations of authority in Australia? With what reasons or emotions do the Australian people clothe their obedience to authority-bearing institutions? For many the answers are loyalty and respectability.

Almost from the colony's start, middle-class respectability has been one of the great religions. It was confronted by a contrary tendency but this, although strong, was generally submerged, usually being allowed into public life only in the arts and entertainments. On 11 November Whitlam had been, in the eyes of many, too much of an entertainer.

Loyalty to the distant monarch was part of this respectability. But the loyalty no longer works in the way the loyalists think it does. Voters who saw Whitlam as 'disloyal' saw themselves as being loyal to Queen Elizabeth. In fact they were being loyal to John Kerr. In reply to a letter to the *Australian* during the election, that we were a 'banana republic', I wrote that we were a 'banana monarchy'. Since beginning to write this book I think a more accurate term is that we are a 'Governor-Generalate'. Most of the organs of authority in Australia are still clothed in the symbols of royalism, or at least of upper-class Britishry, and these give sanctity and magic to a Governor-General who possesses ultimate power. After he acts, they protect him, in that to bring him directly into controversy is to 'involve the Crown'. But the head that wears the crown has nothing to do with his actions, and may even disapprove of them. And a Governor-General can be bolder with an elected government than a monarch: Queen Elizabeth would risk her whole dynasty if she sacked a Prime Minister who then won an election; a Governor-General who backed a loser would be likely to retire into a rich world of company directorates.

Apart from the leftovers of British traditionalism and middle-class respectability, there is also the idea of 'the rules' to excuse authority in Australia, either with the rules themselves abstracted into authority, or with the rules seen as an ideal of fairness.

The rules can appear as an abstract deity giving magic to office-holders. But it is only temporary magic. Office-holders possess the magic of 'the rules' only so long as they hold office. When they lose office they lose their magic. Also, it is only a limited magic. They have only the specific authority that the rules allow. In this way, the idea of 'the rules' sanctifies power by limiting it.

But there is a cruder use of the rules as an abstract authority; the written Constitution was used this way in 1975. One person, the Governor-General, said in effect that he had looked up the rules and they undoubtedly directed him to only one course of action. The sanctity of 'the rules' as interpreted by the Governor-General in his delphic capacity and the sanctity of royalism, with no power left to the actual monarch, provided the basis of power of our Governor-Generalate, on its foundation day, 11 November 1975. Here the rules did not limit the office-holder; the office-holder expanded the rules by giving Queen Elizabeth's authority to *his* interpretation of them.

In their other aspect, 'the rules' can suggest an ultimate belief in the sanctity of human reasonableness. In their reasonable aspect there is potential for fairness; they apply to everybody; they apply predictably; if they seem unsatisfactory there are always prospects that they can be changed. It is here that the idea of 'the rules' approaches some of our ideas of 'democracy'.

But the ideas of 'fairness' and 'democracy' are simply rhetorical devices, self-serving double talk, unless they are specifically defined. Until recently we specifically defined parliamentary democracy to mean that the only institution that gave legitimacy to a government, or could take it away, was the Lower House, itself a legitimate government-maker because it was 'chosen by the people'. (Even if, because of the electoral system, as in 1954, 1961 and 1969 it didn't represent the majority will of the people as measured in votes.)

It is an interesting characteristic of the Australian political system that although 'democracy' is a regular feature of its political rhetoric, none of the official legitimations of authority in Australia are democratic: neither the Constitution, nor any of the symbols or rituals of state. None. I know that some of the greatest crimes against freedom can occur in freedom's name, and that constitutions bursting with democratic aspiration may adorn police-states. Nevertheless this is an interesting characteristic of Australia.

It is interesting partly because at periods when there is a spirit of reform, reform can be easier (or possible) where, as in the United States, democratic themes are stated in a constitution. It is also interesting because the Australian Constitution and the symbols and rituals of state in Australia were influenced by British whimsy; the British, for better or worse, are masters in professing fantasies they know are not true; they are particularly adept at preserving their monarchy so that it can appear to mean everything and in fact means nothing; I don't think John Kerr understood this kind of whimsy.

The complete absence of democratic themes in official

legitimations of authority in Australia is also interesting because there is no glorification in any way at all of the Australian people. The people are not respectable.

There is not much legitimation in Australia of breaking rules for the sake of getting better rules, or of defending rules from arbitrary action. There may still be lying around in the school history texts some fag ends of the old Whig interpretation of British history as a steady growth of freedom coming from various revolts against various kings. Fraser seemed to remember something of this when, having compared Whitlam to Richard III and Falstaff, he then compared him to Charles I. But this all happened in Britain a long time ago. Apart from attempts to do something with the Eureka Stockade, Australians have no legends of reforms gained from their own revolts. They didn't *earn* their political system. It was given to them. At the rally I addressed I saw the blue and white Eureka flags flying among the crowd and the red and white banners calling for a general strike. But they didn't mean anything. They were just bunting.

When Whitlam was sacked by Kerr he went back to the Lodge and drafted a motion to put before Parliament. He didn't act like a figure from British history using modern methods to defend freedom against a tyrant. He didn't ring up Bob Hawke and ask for a general strike. He didn't ring up the Australian Union of Students and ask them to get 10,000 students to picket Government House. He didn't make a speech from the steps of Parliament House saying that the Governor-General had acted against the Constitution and that he would get the House to pass a resolution telling Queen Elizabeth to fire him. Whitlam didn't force a crisis which might have ended in Kerr's resignation, with the appointment of a new Governor-General and the government's survival.

A good reason for not doing so is that it may not have worked. I can't think of any other good reason. Kerr's action was a full assault against parliamentary democracy as it had, by convention, been precisely defined in Australia. Kerr had broken the rules as they were understood by these conventions. If, in 1976, other Australians break rules, because of his action it may be John Kerr's fault.

I am aware of the argument that there is liberty in order. But this can mean that those who exercise forbearance are the losers. One side breaks the rules by redefining them; then the losers are tolerant. The freedom that was won in 1975 was the freedom for the coalition parties to make it easier for themselves to be the natural government in Australia. The Labor Party acquiesced in a change in the political system that has stacked it even more against them.

There is one last question. *Would* Australians ever be ready to act against a Governor-General?

Ten

Death of The Lucky Country

One of the night sisters usually came in with the early morning cup of tea, just before six o'clock. This time she brought a telegram: 'Trust you will join us in a speedy recovery – Gough Whitlam'. I remembered the 1939 University Revue, in my first year at Sydney University. The wittiest act was put on by a law student, E. G. Whitlam.

One way of looking at Whitlam is as a prime minister born to be king. He was a king in the great battles of politics (the parliamentary showing-off, the election campaigns). He was bold like a king, he had favourites like a king, sacked ministers like a king; like a king he got a sinecure for his son. He blamed others like a king, was boastful like a king, sulked like a king. He had the visions of a king, seeking a monopoly on new ambitions, new plans. Like a king, he was ready to protect the poor from the avarice of the merchants and to shock the burghers with the frivolities of art: 'Blue Poles' was a princely purchase. Like a king he was ready to indulge his pleasures blatantly. He walked proudly around foreign archaeological sites in front of the hostile lenses of Australian television cameras. Some of the critics of his international trips spend their leisure time overseas well away from the cameras, with bar-girls or call-girls. If Whitlam had shared their tastes it might still have been difficult to stop him from taking his pleasures in front of the cameras.

This is the point. He was no more tricky, bullying or conniving than his critics, less so than some of them; but like a king he showed off even those qualities. He had no secret faults. He revealed everything about himself, good, bad, amusing, boring. Like a king, he seemed to be in a permanent state

91

of public audience. Or to put it another way, he threw himself on our compassion.

He could repel those he attracted. One side of him appealed to the Australian love of the respectable. He dressed well. He spoke well. He had neat hair. He was a credit to us all. He got us a good name overseas. But the honest, blunt, witty, and sometimes child-like side could offend respectability. He called Malcolm Fraser 'Kerr's cur'. He called Sir Garfield Barwick a 'truculent runt'. He threw a glassful of water at Sir Paul Hasluck.

One side of him was civilized, rational, enlightened, humane. This was the encyclopaedia-reading side. In elections in 1969, 1970, 1972 and 1974 it produced those long, boring lectures on his list of policies; in the 1975 election it produced dissertations on the Constitution. That was the man of the programme, who could seem to approach politics as a careful implementation of good ideas. Yet on his other side there was the style of the crashthrough, the mad itch to throw away reason and give it a go. There was a further complication: even in his rash commitments, or his boasts, he was also, to some unknown extent, sending himself up, an ironist.

He was awkward; despite his facility, he was uncertain in communication. Both wit and crashthrough were ways out of an unbearable silence.

One can make too much of the political importance of Whitlam's personality. His personal popularity could go up and down. In 1975 it began low; it rose; it fell; the election caught him before his popularity recovered – or, as Fraser had hoped, it caught him when his pants were down. When things were going well people could admire, or at least tolerate, aspects of Whitlam that they found intolerable when things were bad. However, both for better and for worse, the Labor government was not just Gough Whitlam. I have spoken of his king-like personality for the special reason that the 1975 defeat made him one of Australia's few political heroes.

There was already an heroic aspect in the three-year struggle of his government, facing not only Senate obstruction, but a Senate-caused election, and then a continuing threat of another Senate-caused election. There was gallantry in the way in which, in this unprecedented condition, Whitlam pushed so much of his programme through. (In this sense the crashthrough style was a sensible tactic.) Then he was assassinated. Then he was assassinated again, by his defeat in an illegitimately called election, done in by strong and powerful enemies. A double martyr, but still living amongst us.

Political heroes don't come easily. That is why there have been so few in Australia, where so many things have come so very easily. For the tens of thousands of people to whom the 1975 election was an opportunity to affirm traditional values which they then saw denied, Whitlam is now a hero. But heroes are created by folk art to stand for something. What does Whitlam stand for? I see him as marking that period in history in which we are witnessing the end of what I called 'the lucky country'.

Let me explain.

When I invented the phrase in 1964 to describe Australia I said 'Australia is a lucky country run by second-rate people who share its luck'. I didn't mean that it had a lot of material resources, although this was how many people used the phrase at the time of euphoria about Australia's mineral exports. Nor did I mean the Bondi Beach syndrome – the lazy burnt-out oaf lying there on the sand until fate caught up with him; I don't mind people lying on the beach. Nor did I mean that Australia had exceptionally high living standards, as these things are measured. Compared with other rich countries, it had begun slowly but steadily sliding down the scale during the Liberal area.

I had in mind the idea of Australia as a derived society whose prosperity in the great age of manufacturing came mainly from the luck of its historical origins. It was sufficiently like the innovative industrial societies of 'the West' to prosper from their innovations; it didn't have to think up much in the way of techniques of design or organization in manufacturing for itself. Nor, more widely, did it show much originality in general social and political changes or world views.

I had in mind in particular the luck lived on by the second-rate, provincial-minded élites of Australia of whom it seemed to me R. G. Menzies was the patron saint. These élites were likely to be affronted by any ideas of unique Australian excellence or even ideas of unique Australian identity (whether in art, foreign affairs, social reforms, or in anything).

The Menzies-style élites were reared in an era of self-congratulation on 'national achievements' that came mainly from foreign innovation, so there was an uneasy basis to their pride. They would claim honour from their connection with foreign money, but they would also demand the honours and the rewards due to initiative and enterprise, even when they had displayed little more than a talent for improvising imitations. There was deliberate dishonesty in some of the denials in 1975 that Australia was part of the world economic crisis, but many people believed this completely. Not having seen Australia's prosperity as merely a side-effect of the prosperity of the affluent world, how could they now see Australia's economic crisis as part of the crisis of the affluent world? It would be to the Labor Party's advantage to learn to dramatize to voters the international character of Australian economic life. It is an essential activity in itself. It could also help win them an election.

The world economic crisis is, in part, a reflection of the end of the great age of manufacturing which reached its peak in the era of affluence. Australia's 'luckiness' was tied to the prosperity of the manufacturing age; declining confidence in manufacturing is the beginning of the end of Australia as the lucky country. As this becomes more painfully evident, even

Menzies's Liberal Party, largely a creation of the age of manufacturing, will have to find another word for 'dole bludger'.

In his emphasis on the service industries, on education, civil amenities, leisure interests, quality of life issues, and in his adventurist lunge at the tariff system, Whitlam was dramatizing the decline in manufacturing supremacy. In this sense he was speeding the lucky country's end.

He also did so (most notably) as a general stirrer. 'Shocks of re-orientation' were forecast (and, in anticipation, applauded) in the book *The Lucky Country*. Whitlam provided them splendidly. In certain ways, although not others, this book may have provided a kind of John the Baptist role for 'Whitlamism', a going-ahead. (A more exact way of putting it is that in some themes they were both part of the same trends.) This is most obvious in the development of new national consciousness during his government, in the elevation of the importance of intelligence and education, in the emphasis on urbanism, and in the assaults he made on racism, Britishry and the world view of the loyal little ally. It is also evident in a desire to catch up with what he called 'comparable countries'. In this sense Whitlam was like a 'modernizer' in a Third World country trying to bring his own people new ideas from overseas.

He was also concerned with the cultivation of an Australian sense of excellence. Aspects of his government included innovations as well as imitations, and it was a government that encouraged innovation in others. If Australians had given the Whitlam government a better run, Australia might have developed something of a name for itself in the world as a humane and progressive nation with a distinctive originality.

It is of great significance that such an ambition was a direct affront to the Menzies-style élites, whose rationale demanded that Australia be second-rate. Menzies's Australia was a banana monarchy. It was a small, loyal Australia that didn't do too much thinking for itself and was important because of its northern hemisphere bigshot friends. The extreme monarchists sneered at Whitlam's 'socialist republic' and so protected themselves against the assaults of possible originality. What was not so obvious was that even many self-styled critics of the Menzies era were also uneasy with ideas of Australia developing its own standards of excellence. They weren't used to such ideas. They didn't know how to handle them. When they made their critiques of Whitlamism, they simply didn't take such strange matters into account. This is one reason why so many estimates of the Whitlam years have been so unjust.

Australia's derivativeness as 'the lucky country' has never been more manifest than in what we are now discovering as the British whimsy of its monarchic Constitution. What we meant by parliamentary democracy in Australia has now been qualified by a new system of government by caprice. Now the less democratically elected House, if controlled by opposing politicians, can sack the government; and the Governor-General, 200 years after 1776, may decide 'at his pleasure' to exercise one or more of the powers of King George III.

In the lucky style, we have never 'earned' our democracy. We simply went along with some British habits, amending them as little as possible. We have never seriously bothered even to teach the forms of our democratic government, such as it is, in schools. We have never put the ideals of democracy into the written Constitution or into the rituals and symbols of state. We do not even consider officially glorifying the Australian people, preferring to glorify royalty and upper-class British traditions insofar as they can be imitated by Australians.

Australians who want at least minimum standards of representativeness in government should commit themselves to 'earning' a new constitution. Not a 'lucky country' constitution, but a democratic constitution, with at least (a) either abolition of the Senate or abolition of its legislative powers, (b) formal recognition that the Prime Minister and the Cabinet exist and that they are chosen only by the House of Representatives, (c) provision for fairer voting (by proportional representation, ideally, even if the Labor Party doesn't like it because it might sometimes force them into coalition), (d) provision for fairer election campaigns, including at least minimum concern with the media, (e) stripping the ceremonial head of state of fanciful powers in case they are used and (f) at the right time, by referendum, declaration of Australia as a republic, an act necessary not only for constitutional reasons, but to hammer home Australia's position on the map, and where its history has so far brought it.

How this is to be achieved, I don't know. Once luck goes, things are harder. One commits oneself, and waits for a chance. Obviously the electoral victors of 1975 are not going to be interested in a new constitution. The old one has served them even better than they expected. Privately they're now boasting that the 1975 election has sewn up the political game for at least nine years, with chances for renewals. And in constitutional change not too much can be expected of the Labor Party, which is a political party, trimming its sails for office. Some of these proposals for reform might embarrass it.

However the Labor Party people should toughen up. They should accept that the lucky country's political system has given them only a small and provisional ration of luck. If the economic crisis washes them back into government in 1978 they should imagine that some of those people who are smiling at them are enemies. Perhaps they should start playing the game the way it has been played against them. They could start by sacking whoever is the Governor-General and putting in someone they can trust. They should command as many of the other heights of power as they can appoint trustworthy people to. They should quickly get a lot of popular reform legislation through the House of Representatives, including electoral reform. If necessary they should gag debate to speed it up. Then as soon as it is twice rejected by the hostile Senate they can call a double dissolution to try and get control of both Houses at a time when popularity is still running their way. If they fail to get control of the Senate they can at least get their electoral reforms and other measures passed by the joint sitting of the two Houses allowed for by the Constitution after a double dissolution. To do this, from the day they achieve office they would have to pay more attention to political cosmetics; in particular they should adopt a group loyalty resilient enough for the media not to be able to present them as a troupe of squabbling clowns, just passing through.

Those Australians who want change will have to do more about it themselves. If the lucky days are gone, part of what is gone is the habit of leaving things to some political party. And we should reject another feature of the lucky days – the habit of using Australian apathy to excuse shrugging off the urge to action. There was something other than 'apathy' in the 1975 election: for many tens of thousands of people the election represented the most intense commitment they had known. That Labor was defeated doesn't mean – as the story is now being spread by some of the Liberals – that Labor 'tried to do too much', that Australians don't want reform. If Australians don't want reform why did they return the Labor Party in the 1974 election?

The only protests I had ever signed before 1975 were manifestos complaining about the treatment of Soviet intellectuals. In the 1974 election I was asked to sign some newspaper ads, but I was fastidious about the wording. In the 1975 election I decided to sign anything, and help in anything. I put my name to seven protests, made a television commercial, wrote pieces for the *Bulletin* and the *Catholic Weekly*, was interviewed on *PM*, the Bob Rogers programme and 2JJ, accepted a number of speaking commitments; and when my eye went I found that, although feeling like an Egyptian mummy swathed in blackness, stared at by people living in the conventional world of the senses, I could still do a bit even with bandages on. Now I am writing this book. There are other things I intend to do.

Sufficient violence was seen to be done to political conventions in Australia in 1975 to raise the question of whether this constitutional violence might be met with physical violence in 1976. 'There'll be blood in the streets', was one of the fears (hopes?) at the end of 1975. Even if all that has happened is an extreme alienation of many Australians from their own political system, this is an example of the incompetence of the coalition parties as conservatives. If a nation has a fairly stable political system, with a wide degree of acceptance, prudent conservatives will not normally take action that a significant number of people may see as an affront to that system, or as pushing a political party outside the system, or as creating martyrs and heroes. Most Labor supporters are used to the idea that a political party can be defeated in an election; they are not accustomed to defeat in what they see as an illegitimately called election after the illegitimate sacking of a government. I would make one guess. It could be a bad year for striking matches: there is a high degree of inflammability.

Knowledge of world politics tells us that reformers who feel cast out of the political system often feel forced to use other methods.

In France there might have been a short, sharp burst in the streets which would have put a Kerr out of office and produced a new constitution. In Australia we have not had these releases.

In the *Australian*, summing up the Whitlam years, Manning Clark said: 'Indeed it may well be that December 13, 1975, will go down in history as that day which converted the radicals from the ballot box to industrial action.' But does this apply to Australia? Manning Clark then added: 'It may be the day which proved once and for all just how hopelessly wedded we, as Australians, are to the petty bourgeois values.'

One can say that if reformers are ready to strike back, they may have to take unusual action. If there are attempts to demystify the Governor-Generalate this will raise questions of tactics not previously considered in Australia. It would be a great reform if the journalists, however mildly, can begin to warm their confidence with some of the ethic of syndicalism; but this is again unusual. If trade unions, by democratic means, decide to engage in new types of political action, and if others, who would not usually do so, support them, that could be the beginning of another new type of achievement. (We should remember that many businesses went on a kind of strike against the Whitlam government, and whether intentionally or unintentionally this helped create the economic climate that they then presented as one of the reasons for getting rid of the Labor government.) If constitutional lawyers and political scientists could get together and draft a democratic Australian constitution, and if its proposals could be crystallized in a few simple principles that were spread widely amongst the people, that might also be a beginning of new action.

Above all, there is a need for discussion to be kept going with an intensity not usual in Australia. It suits the Liberals to spread the idea that the Australian people are apathetic; that there was really no 'constitutional crisis'; or that if there was, it's all forgotten now. That was a line that was begun, and propagandized in the media, right at the beginning of the election campaign. It is in the Liberals' interests that things should stay quiet. They want to be left to sleep it off, like animals after the kill.

Appendix A

Chronology of the Fall of the Whitlam Government

14 October
Prime Minister Whitlam accepts Connor's resignation as Minerals and Energy Minister. Grounds are that Parliament had been misled.

15 October
Editorials in all metropolitan newspapers call on Whitlam to resign. Opposition Leader Fraser announces that the Senate, which he controls, will delay passage of the government's two money Bills until Whitlam calls an election.

16 October
Senate blocks the two money Bills. House of Representatives passes a motion of confidence in the government.

25 October–8 November
Public opinion polls show swing to the government.

10 November
Chief Justice Barwick sees Governor-General Kerr. Later in the day he gives Kerr a letter, which Kerr will subsequently release to justify Whitlam's dismissal.

11 November
9.05am
Whitlam meets Fraser, Lynch, Anthony. Says he will call half-Senate election unless money Bills are passed.
9.50am
Fraser confers with senior members of Shadow Cabinet, then phones Whitlam saying Senate will not pass Bills.

10.00am
Whitlam phones for appointment with Kerr in which he will advise half-Senate election.

10.10am
Whitlam tells Labor caucus there will be half-Senate election.

10.30am
Fraser tells joint meeting of Opposition parties there is nothing to report.

11.45–1.00pm
House of Representatives meets.

12.10pm
Kerr's private secretary phones with message that Fraser is to come to Government House about 1.00pm.

12.45pm
Fraser leaves for Government House, where he is shown into private room.

12.50pm
Whitlam leaves for Government House, not knowing Fraser is there.

1.15pm
Kerr hands Whitlam his letter of dismissal.

1.30pm
Kerr swears Fraser in as Prime Minister.

2.00pm
Government House press handout announces Whitlam's dismissal.

2.00pm
Senate passes money Bills.

2.30pm
Fraser announces he is Prime Minister, moves that the House of Representatives adjourns; is defeated.

3.03pm
Whitlam moves no confidence in Fraser.

3.16pm
House of Representatives passes motion of no confidence in
Fraser. The Speaker asks for appointment with Kerr. Is told
he can't see Kerr till 4.45.
4.50pm
Governor-General's secretary reads proclamation dissolving
Parliament.

24 November
Whitlam opens election campaign.

26 November
Morgan Gallup Poll in the *Bulletin* shows swing against Labor
after Whitlam's dismissal.

13 December
Labor defeated.

Appendix B
Some Relevant Documents

One

Extract from statement made by Prime Minister Whitlam, 15 October, 1975

(He was commenting on the Opposition's decision, announced that day, to use its majority in the Senate to block the government's supply of money and force an election.)

The House of Representatives – the people's House – alone determines who shall govern Australia. Only seventeen months ago, the people for the second time in less than eighteen months, elected the Australian Labor Party to govern for a further three years.

I state again the basic rule of our parliamentary system: governments are made and unmade in the House of Representatives – in the people's House. The Senate cannot, does not, and must never determine who the Government shall be.

That principle has been upheld since Federation. It has never been broken or challenged except during this Government's life. It has been scrupulously observed on at least twenty occasions since Federation when the Opposition had the numbers in the Senate to reject Supply.

Our majority in the House of Representatives has never been threatened. The House of Representatives has passed the Budget. Budgets and all money Bills must originate in the House of Representatives. The Senate cannot even amend them but it can delay them. And this is what Mr Fraser proposes. And how will he do this? By using the numbers in a stacked Senate which is not even the same Senate which the people elected only seventeen months ago.

It is in the words of Mr Killen, the Liberal member for Moreton in Queensland, 'a tainted Senate'. In May 1974 the people of Australia elected a Senate in which the Government had twenty-nine senators and the Liberal and Country Party also had twenty-nine senators. There were two Independents. The Labor Party – the government – received 200,000 votes in the elections for the Senate over all our opponents combined.

But because two State premiers flouted another great constitutional convention the Government now has only twenty-seven senators.

It is this unrepresentative Senate, this tainted Senate, which Mr Fraser intends to use as a weapon to strike down the democratically elected Government of Australia – to render it incapable of carrying out the programme which it was elected to carry out.

Two

Extracts from advice given to the Governor-General by Solicitor-General M. H. Byers, 4 November 1975

(Released 19 November 1975 by Mr Kep Enderby, Attorney-General in the Whitlam government and co-signer of the advice.)

Mr Byers had been asked to give a legal opinion on the statement of Mr R. J. Ellicott (who was to become Attorney-General in the Fraser government) that the Governor-General was 'legally obliged' to take action once the Senate blocked supply. This view of Mr Ellicott's was similar to the one later adopted by the Governor-General. Mr Byers took a different view.

These are three key extracts from his opinion:

Section 61 affords no ground for the conclusion that upon the Senate deferring, or rejecting, Supply solely to procure the resignation or dismissal of the ministry possessing a majority in the Representatives, His Excellency is constitutionally obliged immediately to seek an explanation of the Prime Minister of how he proposes to overcome that situation.

Nor do we agree with the suggestion, that were the Prime Minister unable to suggest means which solved the disagreement between the Houses and left the Government without funds to carry on, it would be His Excellency's duty to dismiss his ministers.

We do not suggest that, should a case exist for his intervention, His Excellency, in considering the course he will take, must disregard the fact that the Senate's deferring or refusing of Supply will impede the business of the Government. We do suggest that His Excellency is not confined to a consideration of that fact. He may consider others. After all the constitutional provisions but recognise that the ministry holds office during His Excellency's pleasure (Section 64) and that he may dissolve the Representatives before the expiry of its term (Sections 28 and 5); they do not, considered alone, afford any guide as to the circumstances when the extreme and abnormal reserve powers of dismissal of a ministry and consequent dissolution of the Representatives, should or may be exercised or even that they still exist. This is the field of convention and discretion.

But it is we think, not correct to treat the exercise of those powers as demanded when refusal of Supply is threatened or when it occurs. To do so is to deny, for example a Vice Regal authority to offer suggestions where the circumstances have reached a stage sufficiently grave to warrant His Excellency's adoption of that course, bearing in mind that the cardinal rule is that the Crown should not 'withdraw these differences from their proper sphere' . . .

The Senate's resolution indicates an intention to defer passage of the Appropriation Bill until either the Ministry resigns or the Governor-General acting against his advice dismisses it and, upon advice of ministers in the minority of Representatives, dissolves it.

The Ministry has not resigned and will not do so. That means only a forced dissolution. Dr Jennings' (Cabinet Government, 3rd ed., 1969) observes (page 403) that 'no government has been dismissed by the Sovereign since 1783', and points out that there was no dismissal in 1834 of Lord Melbourne's Government (pages 403–405).

Dr Forsey (The Royal Power of Dissolution of Parliament, 1943) says that 'In the overseas empire there appears to have been only one instance of this: New Brunswick in 1853' (page 71). The passage continues:

'The dissolution in Newfoundland in 1861, New Brunswick in 1866, Quebec in 1878 and 1891, British Columbia in 1900, Queensland in 1907, and NSW in 1932, like the British dissolution of 1807, were not true forced dissolutions.

108

'Ministers were not dismissed because they "refused to advise dissolution; they were dismissed for quite other reasons, and dissolutions granted to their successors because they could not hope to carry on government with the existing Lower House".

'We have referred to forced dissolutions only to indicate that their very rarity and the long years since their exercise passed the gravest doubt upon the present existence of that prerogative'. . .

There is, or is threatening, a legislative deadlock. Section 57 of the Constitution enshrines the Constitutional solution 'of the spectre of legislative deadlock' which possession by the Senate of the power to reject legislation including money bills necessarily gave rise to.

The Section 'relies, after the first occurrence of deadlock, upon providing opportunity for second and perhaps wider thoughts and for negotiation and compromise between the chambers'.

If such be the Section's purpose and intended operation, how is it possible consistently with the Constitution that a reserve power of uncertain existence and unknowable constituents must be exercised in a way necessarily denying effect to the one constitutional provision expressly directed to the solution of deadlock between the Houses? We do not find it possible ourselves to accept that view and to the extent that Mr Ellicott does so he is, we think, clearly wrong.

Three

Letter from Chief Justice Barwick to the Governor-General, 10 November 1975

(Released by the Governor-General, 18 November 1975)

Dear Sir John

In response to Your Excellency's invitation I attended this day at Admiralty House. In our conversations I indicated that I considered myself, as Chief Justice of Australia, free, on Your Excellency's request, to offer you legal advice as to Your Excellency's constitutional rights and duties in relation to an existing situation which, of its nature, was unlikely to come before the court. We both clearly understood that I was not in any way concerned with matters of a purely political kind, or with any political consequences of the advice I might give.

In response to Your Excellency's request for my legal advice as to whether a course on which you had determined was consistent with your constitutional authority and duty, I respectfully offer the following.

The Constitution of Australia is a Federal Constitution which embodies the principle of ministerial responsibility. The Parliament consists of two Houses, the House of Representatives and the Senate, each popularly elected, and each with the same legislative power, with the one exception that the Senate may not originate nor amend a money Bill.

Two relevant constitutional consequences flow from this structure of the Parliament. First, the Senate has Constitutional power to refuse to pass a money Bill; it has power to refuse Supply to the Government of the day. Secondly, a Prime Minister who cannot ensure Supply to the Crown, including funds for carrying on the ordinary services of government, must either advise a General Election (of a kind which the constitutional situation may then allow) or resign. If, being unable to secure Supply, he refuses to take either course, Your Excellency has constitutional authority to withdraw his commission as Prime Minister.

There is no analogy in respect of a Prime Minister's duty between the situation of the Parliament under the Federal Constitution of Australia and the relationship between the House of Commons, a popularly elected body, and the House of Lords, a non-elected body, in the unitary form of Government functioning in the United Kingdom. Under that system, a Government having the confidence of the House of Commons can secure supply, despite a recalcitrant House of Lords.

But it is otherwise under our Federal Constitution.

A Government having the confidence of the House of Representatives but not that of the Senate, both elected Houses, cannot secure Supply to the Crown.

But there is an analogy between the situation of a Prime Minister who has lost the confidence of the House of Commons and a Prime Minister who does not have the confidence of the Parliament, i.e. of the House of Representatives and of the Senate. The duty and responsibility of the Prime Minister to the Crown in each case is the same: if unable to secure Supply to the Crown, to resign or to advise an election.

In the event that, conformably to this advice, the Prime Minister ceases to retain his commission, Your Excellency's Constitutional authority and duty would be to invite the Leader of the Opposition, if he can undertake to secure Supply, to form a Caretaker Government (i.e. one which makes no appointments or initiates any policies) pending a General Election, whether of the House of Representatives, or of both Houses of the Parliament, as that Government may advise.

Accordingly, my opinion is that, if Your Excellency is satisfied in the current situation that the present Government is unable to secure Supply, the course upon which Your Excellency has determined is consistent with your constitutional authority and duty.

Yours respectfully,
Garfield Barwick

Four

Letter of dismissal from the Governor-General to the Prime Minister, 11 November 1975

Dear Mr Whitlam

In accordance with Section 64 of the Constitution, I hereby determine your appointment as my Chief Adviser and Head of the Government.

It follows that I also hereby determine the appointments of all of the Ministers in your Government.

You have previously told me that you would never resign or advise an election of the House of Representatives or a Double Dissolution and that the only way in which such an election could be obtained would be by my dismissal of you and your ministerial colleagues.

As it appeared likely that you would today persist in this attitude, I decided that, if you did, I would determine your commission and state my reasons for doing so.

You have persisted in your attitude and I have accordingly acted as indicated.

I attach a statement of my reasons which I intend to publish immediately.

It is with a great deal of regret that I have taken this step, both in respect of yourself and your colleagues.

I propose to send for the Leader of the Opposition and to commission him to form a new caretaker Government until an election can be held.

Yours sincerely,
(Sgd) John R. Kerr

Five

Statement of reasons given by the Governor-General for dismissing the Whitlam government, 11 November 1975

It has been necessary for me to find a democratic and constitutional solution to the current crisis which will permit the people of Australia to decide as soon as possible what should be the outcome of the deadlock which developed over Supply between the two Houses of Parliament and between the Government and the Opposition parties.

The only solution consistent with the Constitution and with my oath of office and my responsibilities, authority and duty as Governor-General is to terminate the commission as Prime Minister of Mr Whitlam and to arrange for a caretaker government able to secure Supply and willing to let the issue go to the people.

I shall summarize the elements of the problem and the reasons for my decision which places the matter before the people of Australia for prompt determination.

Because of the Federal nature of our Constitution and because of its provisions the Senate undoubtedly has constitutional power to refuse or defer Supply to the Government. Because of the principles of responsible government a Prime Minister who cannot obtain Supply, including money for carrying on the ordinary services of government, must either advise a general election or resign.

If he refuses to do this I have the authority, and indeed the duty, under the Constitution to withdraw his commission as Prime Minister.

The position in Australia is quite different from the position in the United Kingdom. Here the confidence of both Houses on Supply is necessary to ensure its provision. In the United Kingdom the confidence of the House of Commons alone is necessary.

But both here and in the United Kingdom the duty of the

114

Prime Minister is the same in a most important respect – if he cannot get Supply he must resign or advise an election.

If a Prime Minister refuses to resign or to advise an election, and this is the case with Mr Whitlam, my constitutional authority and duty require me to do what I have now done – to withdraw his commission and to invite the Leader of the Opposition to form a caretaker government – that is, one that makes no appointments or dismissals and initiates no policies, until a general election is held. It is most desirable that he should guarantee Supply. Mr Fraser will be asked to give the necessary undertakings and advise where he is prepared to recommend a double dissolution. He will also be asked to guarantee Supply.

The decisions I have made were made after I was satisfied that Mr Whitlam could not obtain Supply. No other decision open to me would enable the Australian people to decide for themselves what should be done.

Once I had made up my mind, for my own part, what I must do if Mr Whitlam persisted in his stated intentions I consulted the Chief Justice of Australia, Sir Garfield Barwick. I have his permission to say that I consulted him in this way.

The result is that there will be an early general election for both Houses and the people can do what, in a democracy such as ours, is their responsibility and duty and theirs alone. It is for the people now to decide the issue which the two leaders have failed to settle.

(Sir John then gave a detailed statement of his decision which was fully reprinted in the daily press of 12 November 1975.)

The Lucky Country

Donald Horne

No one has dissected Australia with such stylish
ruthlessness and native wit as Donald Horne in
The Lucky Country. Outselling all other books on
Australia by far, it has become part of the society it sets
out to explore, and the phrase 'the lucky country' has
become part of the Australian language. This book is
indispensable to an understanding of contemporary
Australia.

The Education of Young Donald

Donald Horne

The classic autobiography of a well-known Australian, *The Education of Young Donald* is both the personal story of one man in the twenties and thirties and the story of an entire generation.

'It is, with very little doubt, one of the most living and enduring of Australian biographies.'
– Max Harris

'It is a very good book indeed; all, or very nearly all, that an autobiography should be.'
– *New Statesman*